CLIMATE CHANGE

BE PREPARED

A Convenient Truth That We All Need to Know

Marshall Clayton

Climate Change: Be Prepared
Copyright © 2024 by Marshall Clayton

ISBN
978-1-963254-45-7 (Paperback)
978-1-963254-46-4 (eBook)
978-1-963254-44-0 (Hardcover)

Dedication

This book is dedicated to the memory of Claybourne Faircloth, my former pastor and the man that was preaching the Sunday I was saved.

His passion for truth and desire to share that truth from God's word still inspires me to this present day.

Through his preaching I leaned to never just take any man at his word concerning truth but to seek God's Spirit realizing that he is the only true teacher as it relates to God's word.

As you read this book it's my prayer that you might see that same passion and still allow God's Spirit be the person that teaches truth.

TABLE OF CONTENTS

Prologue vii

Chapter 1   Climate Change: Purpose 1

Chapter 2   Climate Change: Time until the First 5

Chapter 3   Climate Change: What We Think We Know 11

Chapter 4   The First Climate Change Forecaster 16

Chapter 5   Climate Change: Is It Possible? 22

Chapter 6   What's Real? 27

Chapter 7   When Jesus Gave up the Ghost 34

Chapter 8   End of Your Time: My Time 40

Chapter 9   Israel's Time 47

Chapter 10   When God the Father Promises 53

Chapter 11   Climate Change: The Church Is Gone 62

Chapter 12   King of Kings, Lord of Lords 71

Chapter 13   It's Over: The Ark Has Settled 76

Chapter 14   Closing Thoughts: Truth 81

PROLOGUE

Anything I might say here would be what I used to be. All that is very unimportant. I will say that I love to write, but I don't consider myself to be an author. What I desire is for each person to see and recognize who I am now. That's a person with a great passion for sharing the gospel truth with this sin-cursed world. We live in a time of great deception, when very little real truth is ever revealed. My desire is to allow God's Spirit to speak to you through what I write and prepare each person to stand before God one day!

I often tell people that I'm not educated. Actually, as far as this world is concerned, you have absolutely no reason to listen to or read anything I might say. The truth is, I seek to create a situation where it's actually God's Spirit you hear speak to your heart as you read what I write.

It's something we often forget. We see people win all kinds of rewards, titles and so on. Many people are highly esteemed in this world in many different ways. However, when we stand before God, we'll all be standing on equal ground! Therefore, for the sake of argument, I will place myself far below you as an individual. As I do that, you can decide who I am and my worthiness to be seen or recognized in the world we live in. After all, it actually doesn't matter who any of us are, but rather, who do we represent? And, I might add, just how well?

In the end, what are you reaching for?

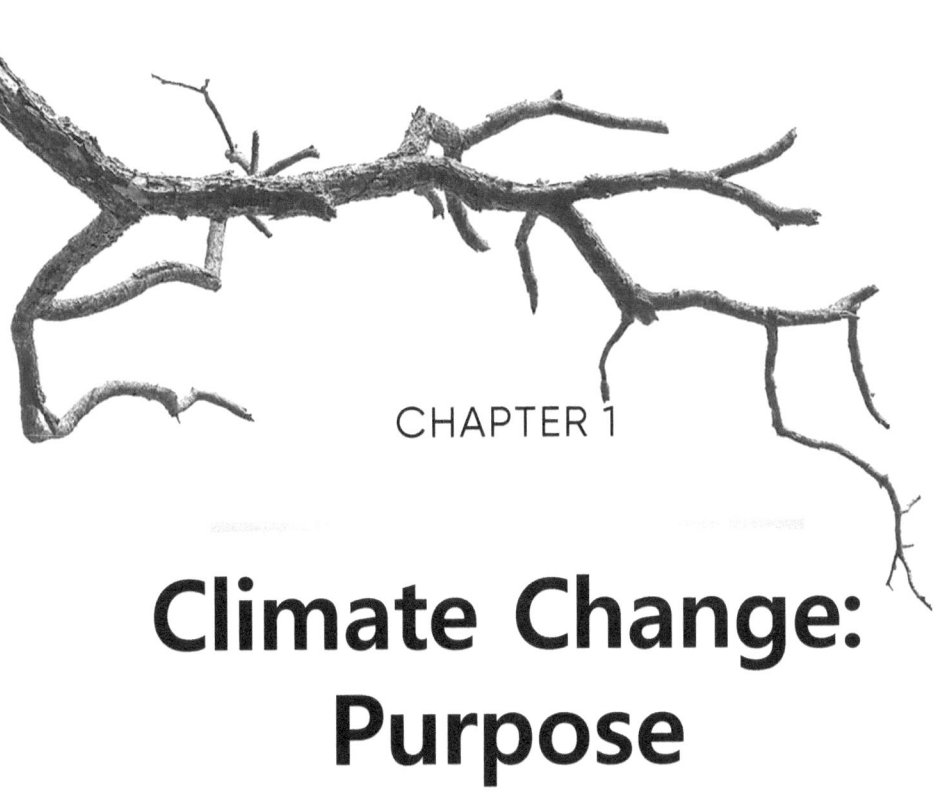

CHAPTER 1

Climate Change: Purpose

What should you believe? To whom should you listen? These questions can only be answered by you. There is an absolute truth. The question might be, *But where can I find it?* Well, if you are searching for an absolute in science, you can't ask me, or an absolute in math, I don't know. I can't even say that I can give you absolutes about climate change; however, I can say that you and I can find absolute truth in God's Holy Word. We just have to be willing to find it. The truth about climate change and the details around it are in that book.

God deals with people as individuals, such as you and me.

There are churches, communities, countries, and all kinds of organizations that might do great things, but God, through the power of the Holy Spirit, speaks to individuals. His voice is heard through the mouth of all those who seek absolutes in their lives, such as the truth in his book, the Bible.

There are some absolute things we know. Most people understand gravity—if you fall, you hit the ground. Two plus two equals four, and so on. Things such as these are taught to us by people who have a passion for teaching. Some we might learn simply by trial and error.

As we mature, we learn these absolutes. The education that teaches these things might even be forced on us to some degree. While this is true, the Word of God is not a book that we have to study or read; therefore, many of us neglect to seek the absolutes in scripture. We learn what we know about scripture for someone else that we deem more likely to know and have the ability to understand it.

The absolute truth, as seen in scripture, is that God's desire is to speak to you and teach you without the aid of any other person.

God, through the power of his spirit, uses other people to teach and instruct, but only so that you might learn to hear his voice, to hear absolute truth from him. God's desire is to have a very personal relationship with you—a relationship that brings comfort and peace to your heart in a troubled world. As he walks with you, your knowledge of him and confidence in his ability to keep you safe no matter what happens in this world increases by leaps and bounds. Finding the truth will have that effect.

Far too often, we depend entirely on other people's opinions and take them as absolute truth when in reality, it's not wise to do so.

The purpose of this book is to try and point each reader in the direction that we need to look for correct answers. I will add, as I do in most things I write, that in reality, it's not myself whom I desire for you to hear when I write.

There's a power much bigger than I, or any other person, will ever be. He lives in the hearts of the people who will allow him to live there. His desire is to teach and lead all people into righteousness.

That power is the Holy Spirit of God. He only deals with the truth.

As I try to lay out biblical climate change, it's still up to you to find the truth. The truth is settling. The truth brings peace of mind.

In all that I write or say, I cannot give you those things, nor can any other person. By the same token, God, through the power of the Holy Spirit, can.

My desire is to reveal the truth, as given by him, that you can grow thereby.

Every person has an opinion. While that is true, opinion, even if it's mine, is not what we need. We need to understand truth, and that just as close as possible without any man's opinion. The word of God is not an opinion; it's the truth. We, you and I, just have to study and find it.

Faith is the substance of things hoped for and the evidence of things not seen (Hebrews 11:1). I can't see those things that happened before I was born. I also can't see what will happen when I am gone. By faith, I believe in the biblical truth about our past and our future.

As you read this book, let's try together to come to an understanding of real climate change. As I write, all will be based on God's Word. To the best of my ability, it will have nothing to do with my opinion.

We are taught, in some cases and by some people, that scripture can be interpreted differently by different people who might read the same scripture. The interpretation might be different, but we must understand that there is but one truth. When I find that my interpretation is wrong through my own personal study or because of the teaching of another who is seeking truth, then I must be willing to change my interpretation to factual truth.

My faith is steadfast and settled entirely in God's Word. My desire is to help everyone who reads this book to better understand how time and climate change is unfolding and why.

For a number of reasons, we live in a world where history is being hidden from us. What is behind humanity is being rewritten. We have allowed our history books and our Bibles to be closed while our minds are being filled with obscure thoughts of the common man.

While that is very true in the secular world, it is also being destroyed in the spiritual realm as well. In our churches, history is little spoken of, and the teaching of former events is seldom studied.

The Bible, God's Holy Word, not only helps us to see history but also opens our eyes to future events as well. Satan knows that if he can close our eyes and keep us from seeing history, then things that will unfold in the future will be hidden as well.

As I say this, I realize that I am just a man, an individual whom, actually, not one person has any reason to believe in. It's my desire that God, through the power of the Holy Spirit, may use what I write to open the reader's understanding of scripture. My prayer is that it will create a thought process, a desire to study and learn far beyond my ability to teach, in each person who reads this book.

I will also be the first to admit that I am not always correct in my understanding, nor am I a great author. With that being said, if I can get you to study God's Holy Word, then we all can grow together.

Be not deceived. Biblically speaking, global warming and climate change are real. We just have to understand why and when it will be. Therefore, let's get started.

Let's allow God to speak, to teach, to instruct each of us. As you read, study around me, prove the things I say whether I'm right or wrong. If we follow that course, then to God be the glory. He must increase in each of us. His knowledge is power. His truth will set us free.

If we as individuals can be set free from the deceptions of this world and educated by the true God of this universe, then within that, we find the power of unity, each individual being taught and led by the same spirit. In reality, God and one is a majority. The god of truth and you is that majority. If that God is for us, then who can stand against us?

CHAPTER 2

Climate Change: Time until the First

The study of God's Word is fascinating. We, in most cases, look at it as confusing and as a lot of unimportant writings that we don't need. We see it as boring. I confess, some of it is to me as well.

The one thing that is missed in some cases is the presence of the Holy Spirit in our lives. Many try to understand God's word without first being born into his family. This is the first and foremost. The Word of God is spiritually discerned. Man cannot understand it, nor can they teach it unless they have the spirit of God within them (1 Corinthians 2:14). Now, as I make that statement, you don't know that I have that spirit within me, do you?

We cannot judge that one simple point about another person; therefore, it's up to each individual to know if that spirit lives within them, then to weigh what they read or hear in the light of God's spirit within themselves.

If we have God's spirit within our own bodies, then that spirit will help us discern what we read or hear from someone else, whether it is driven by God's spirit or another spirit.

I make those remarks because of the things I am about to say. Therefore, you must weigh what I say and allow God's spirit to help you make up your mind about the possibility that I am right.

Global warming or climate change is a fact of life. It has occurred and will occur again. Although there were people here when it happened the first time, and people will be here to witness it the next time, it's quite possible that the people here now will not be living at the time of the next climate change. However, preparation is still important.

When we speak of global warming, we mean just that—over the whole globe.

Although God destroyed the things of this earth by water the last time, he promised us that he would not destroy it again by water. When you see a rainbow, that is a symbol of that promise. He made a covenant with Noah and placed the rainbow there as a constant reminder to us of that covenant (Genesis 9:10–19). That's another first. There had never been a rainbow before the flood because it never rained.

One question that we need to consider is, how was this earth before that flood happened? What's the difference between that time and the way it is now? And will it go back to what it was? I know those are three questions, but let's seek to find answers.

Let's look at some things we know. Adam, in the Garden of Eden, worked or attended to all the animals that God had created. There was no fear of them by him, nor did one animal fear another. All the animals must have had a gentle nature and were easily managed.

Noah even put those same animals on the ark some years later. During the entire time they were on the ark, there weren't any killings or fighting. Something must have changed drastically as soon as they came off the ark. There's no way you could put all those animals together on a boat today and expect them all to survive. We see here where the animals changed once they left the ark (Genesis 9:2). Before, they were tame and easily brought onto the ark, but now they fear Noah. That fear of men still remains in animals until the days in which we live. I'd like to point out something here that I think we can consider. We just never think about it. Just how easy was it to communicate with the animals before the flood? Look at this verse from Genesis 3:1: "Now the serpent was more subtil than any beast of the field which the LORD God had made. And he said unto the woman, Yea, hath God said, Ye shall not eat of every tree of the garden?"

I only point this out because Eve seemed very comfortable communicating with the serpent, even speaking the same language. Was that a common practice in the Garden of Eden?

How well did man and animals communicate? Just another question that we have no answer to, but it might show us just how much things changed after the flood.

We know that when Adam and Eve left the Garden of Eden, the earth became sin-cursed. We also see that the ability to sin was in the garden. It only took deception to bring it out.

We also know that after they left the garden, sin became so bad that God decided to destroy every living thing, but Noah found grace in the eyes of the Lord (Genesis 6:8). If we look at a spiritual fact here that is common to our everyday lives, we can learn something.

Sin, when it is committed, seems harmless enough, but when it is finished, it brings death (James 1:15). God told Adam that he would have to work, that it was a by-product of the sin he committed, that they also had to leave the Garden of Eden. We can read this account in Genesis 3, especially in verse 24. God placed an angel (cherubim) at the gate of Eden to keep them away from the tree of life. The point is that in the beginning, after leaving the garden, it didn't seem so bad, just as sin and lust in our lives seem good when committed. We can't see the destruction until a later date.

The earth was still the same, and all seemed well. We see that it was even possible to find and return into the Garden of Eden, but it was protected by an angel.

Just as many people think, things will always be the way they are today; the people of that day assumed the same thing: the animals were friendly, the grass was still green, and, more than likely, Adam had not begun to have to work at that point. The way it appears, Adam and Eve actually died, never seeing any real change other than children being born and the earth outside the Garden of Eden showing sin and cursedness.

Do you realize that there were no children born in the Garden of Eden? Adam and Eve began to have children after they left the garden. Sin began to multiply, and evil was everywhere. Basically, man had forgotten the very God that created him. It was all about the self and what was good in man's eyes (Genesis 6:1–7). Does this mind-set of man sound familiar to you? The Bible also says that in the day of the coming of the Lord, it would be as in the days of Noah (Matthew 23:37). Again, Noah preached for 120 years; no one listened. They didn't believe things would ever change. When we least expect it, destruction comes. Are we not in the same place today? We have every available opportunity to seek out Jesus, but it all falls on self-loving ears. This might be pointed out a little later, but it needs to be seen here as well. Noah was in the spiritual line in scripture. We see sin as it multiplies on earth here, but God has always had a man or a person to represent; we might say, today, that spiritual line is in the body of Jesus Christ. Each person who asks him to be their savior is in that same line. The people of that day before the flood had to prove their belief by getting on the ark, maybe helping to build it. Today we accept Jesus Christ and build a testimony for him.

Sin runs rampant when men allow it in their flesh. It takes self-control and a spirit that willingly yields to his spirit to control the weakness of sin in our flesh. The Bible says that their every thought was to do evil. Mankind forgot God, the creator of everything.

God created earth, and it was perfect. He formed man in his own image. The problem came with man, the weakness of his flesh and his willingness to yield to that weakness.

The earth stayed the same as God created it, even the Garden of Eden did, until the flood came. Remember how subtle the serpent was? Change, sometimes, is that way as well. Things begin to change, but it's so subtle that we never notice it. Here a little, there a little, and the first thing you know, we can't even see God in what we do at all. More than likely, some of those people had good intentions; many probably trusted in some form of God but just could not bring themselves to believe Noah.

When Noah and his family settled back on earth after the flood, they met a whole new place; the old earth was gone.

You have to understand that from the exit of Eden until the flood, all things remained pretty much the same on earth, everything that is, except the one thing that should not have changed—their walk with God. If you were to believe that the things of this earth would ever change from the landscape of that day, it would have to be by faith—faith in what Noah preached.

The only man whom we see who had that faith was Noah. His family also believed and was prepared to meet God.

Although God destroyed the earth with water that day, he promised that he would never destroy it with water again. He placed a rainbow in the sky as a token of his promise. Every time you see a rainbow, you can be assured of that promise (Genesis 9:12–17). This world will never be completely destroyed by water again.

Here, we see real climate change.

That was some four thousand years ago. Basically, for that period, things have remained the same. I'm sure that over the years, we could document some noticeable changes, maybe in weather patterns and maybe in the location of rivers. Some changes can be expected. Change, to some degree, happens every day, but as an earth-noticing fact, most things have remained the same.

Climate change, which is real and very noticeable, is coming again, just as it did in Noah's day. Just as every individual should have prepared for that climate change, every individual must prepare for this one for themselves. We cannot tell exactly when it will occur, but just as that climate change was foretold, so is the next one.

Most of these things are easily proven if you have faith in God's Word.

So we answered, to some degree, two of the questions. However, there will always be questions. The joy is seeking and finding answers, and that is revealed by God's spirit to you as an individual. We will never be able to have all our questions answered in this side of eternity. The secret is knowing the one person who knows all the answers. Then as you walk and talk to him, all the unanswered ones won't matter as much. The reason for that is that one day, on the other side of the climate change before us, we'll know all the answers because we know him.

The one question that remains is, *Will the earth go back to what it was before the flood?*

The next chapter will start a journey through a sin-cursed world. Noah and his family had faith. That doesn't mean they were sin-free. Each person on the ark, although they had faith and were saved, still had the sin's curse on their lives, just as we do today. The whole earth has changed; now, with that change and the sin's curse, choices have to be made.

As we go through this, there are so many things I see to teach. My heartfelt desire is to show why climate change happened then and why it's coming again. Just as God's desire was for people to believe then, he still has that same desire for each of us today.

"Study to show thyself approved unto God, a workman who needeth not to be ashamed, rightly dividing the word of truth" (2 Timothy 2:15).

You study, learn, and allow God to lead your own heart.

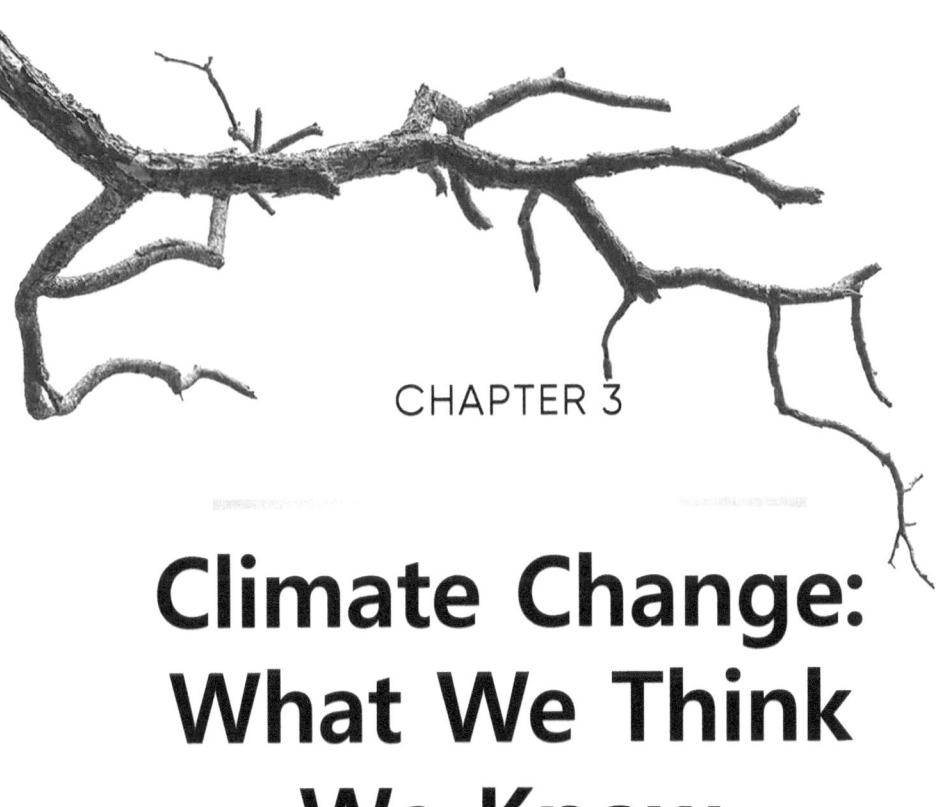

CHAPTER 3

Climate Change: What We Think We Know

We look at our world today with all its development and what mankind has been able to accomplish. When I speak of *we (as in the chapter title)*, I guess maybe it's not really so many, they are the people who consider what I am about to say. At any rate, some people think we are more civilized than any people before us, but are we? Why is it that many people will listen to someone who develops a way to tell how old a bone is or how long the earth has been here, maybe even how they think it was formed, but never take the time to see what God has to say about it? Do you realize that you are placing faith in something or someone either way?

God, in his word, gives us little things to help us know little things. I don't know that it matters that much as far as our future. By that, I mean *eternal future*. I'm just a man, nothing special. Very few people even know me. But in reality, I'm no different from any other person. I'll live, and then I'll die. The most important thing I'll ever do is prepare myself for that eternity.

We see in Genesis that Adam and Eve had two sons, Cain and Abel. Cain killed Abel, and afterward, they were blessed with a son to replace Abel; his name was Seth. You can read the story. The only reason I tell that story is to make a point. Many people will ask this question: *Who did Cain marry?* It always fascinated me why they were concerned about who Cain married but never asked about Seth.

More than likely, if you hear that question asked, the person asking is simply repeating a question they heard from someone else.

It's possible they don't even know he had a brother named Seth or any of the stories about them.

In reality, they never took the time to seek an answer from God's word.

The answer, more than likely, is he married his sister; if not his sister, maybe a niece. If you continue to read the scripture and get over to the genealogy part in Genesis, you will see how long Adam lived and that he had other sons and daughters.

Men seek answers from other men. The truth is that each of us should seek answers from God through his word and by his spirit. We can seek answers from men, but we should always weigh them according to God's word.

What we think we know, in some cases, will show just how little we really know. I find that to be the case often with my very mind-set.

These things we see in Genesis 4 also tell us what some of Adam's family did for a living, such as playing the harp and working with iron and brass. This was just in the first few hundred years after the beginning of man. I wonder just how much were they like to what we are now before God destroyed the earth with water. We assume that we have progressed from the beginning into what we are today. I truly believe that man has done great things that we simply would not believe if we really knew all they had done.

In just a few years after the flood, man had developed to the point that they attempted to build a tower to heaven. God came down and confounded their language. He caused men to speak different languages to slow them down. We see that in Genesis 11.

Some things we see in scripture teach or may show us small looks into the past. We just have to seek God's will and have a heart that desires to see those things. We readily believe things that men show us today, as if their ability to look into the past by science is the only way to know things.

In reality, God's way, his method, is much more effective. It's also much less stressful. For instance, since I believe in God and, by faith, accept his account of history, how much more do I really need to know?

Man says dinosaurs used to live on earth. I see the evidence of that, and I believe they did. But beyond that, as far as where I will spend eternity, it doesn't matter, does it?

We allow what we think, and we can assume from the past, to take priority over our desire to know God and his love for us. We spend our time on other studies when, in reality, our life will soon be over, and what we should have been preparing for is far from being settled.

Every person with a developing mind has some kind of interest. There is nothing wrong with that aspect of our lives. It's human nature to seek understanding of things, the vastness of the universe, the depth of the sea, and even where we came from. All those things are what bring excitement to our lives. However, it must never become something that is bigger in our lives than the truth and the reality that we must prepare to meet God.

As we move forward and learn and even decide our passions, we are overwhelmed by men of similar passions. This will be true no matter what your passions are. Even reading this can be an influence; words written by me or any person can sway and influence. The greatest teacher will always be the Holy Spirit of God. He, the spirit, desires to live within your heart. As I write, I always try to make the point that, in reality, it's not myself whom I desire for you to hear but rather that spirit that is placed within you by God the Father.

There are some things that we can prove in scripture; other things are not so simple. My opinion will always be just my opinion. My desire is for any person to take it as just that. As we try to use scripture as a guide to truth, which is where we find the true baseline, then that's not opinion. Many people struggle with having faith and putting confidence in the book we call the Bible. The truth is that we all die, no matter what we do on this earth; there is something beyond we must prepare for. These things we know. Be careful in whom you trust and in whom you allow to set your overall mindset; that even includes me.

We started this chapter by speaking of Adam's two sons, Cain and Abel. Cain killed Abel (Genesis 4). We saw the things men were able to learn and do. All these things were done by the descendants of Cain. The two sons we see in scripture represent the two natures of mankind. The first is the physical nature, being Cain, and the second is the spiritual nature, being Abel.

As we look at this, we see that all the worldly things and the ability to build them were done by the physical or natural man, not the spiritual man.

We will see a little later when Eve has another son named Seth, that replaces the spiritual man that Cain slew.

The spiritual man is the central focus in scripture; that family line is the one we watch unfold as we walk through all the studies.

The reason for the first climate change was because man followed his own desires and not the desires of the spiritual aspect of their lives.

The spiritual line of the people in that day wasn't to do the things of this world or enjoy their passions but to focus on the will of God.

They all had to work, eat, and care for their families just as we do, but they allowed God to lead their hearts as they worked and enjoyed the lives they lived. We saw Noah working and building as he followed God's will.

The point is that we simply assume that those people of that day were not as far advanced as we are; maybe not, but it's a possibility they knew more than we thought.

Men of this world become wise in their own conceits; they leave God out of their whole mindset, and at that, they become foolish. "Seest thou a man wise in his own conceit? There is more hope of a fool than of him" (Proverbs 26:12).

All the knowledge that exists without the wisdom that we gain through God's Word and by the Holy Spirit, if to no avail, might achieve greatness in this world, but it draws us no closer to a relationship with God the Savior.

The people of Noah's day had the knowledge and, probably, the wisdom of this world. They knew how to make and play harps; they worked with brass and iron. There is no way to tell just how intelligent they had become. The problem was that they did it without the saving knowledge of God. Noah was foolish to them. Noah might have been the least esteemed person, and that included his family, but who was the wisest in the end?

What you think you know, no matter what position you hold in this life, is all vain without a relationship with Jesus Christ. We work and build; we gain wealth, knowing at the same time that death and the end is coming. Although the people of Noah's day lived a lot longer than we would do, they also knew that at some point, all men must die. And at that, we must face the same righteous God whom Noah preached about. What we think we know now might be to our own demise if we walk without God.

CHAPTER 4

The First Climate Change Forecaster

In the world we live in today, we hear a lot about climate change. There are those who say that it's happening right before our eyes. On the one hand, they tell us what we need to do to correct it or at least slow it down. On the other hand, there are people who say it's not happening. It's just an ongoing debate about what man can or cannot do about climate change.

These people who are trying to prepare us for climate change are not the first people to speak of this change that can and will happen in the world we live in. There was a man named Noah in the Word of God—in the first book, the book of Genesis—who proclaimed the same thing. We can start to read about him in Genesis 6 and a few chapters after. God spoke to him and told him to build an ark for salvation from the coming climate change. Why build an ark? It had never rained. There had never been a cloud in the sky; we could even speculate that, seeing that everything was watered from beneath.

Very seldom do we hear today about the fact that in the beginning, it never rained, that is, no water of any kind fell from the sky like we see today. Even when we use the Bible as a teaching tool, we don't look back that far in history or study to understand those things that we use to teach on a regular basis. But there in Genesis, we find that climate change is the vehicle that created the drastic change that started the very weather, even the seasons we see today.

In the beginning, there were rivers and streams, but everything was watered from beneath the earth. One river started in Eden and split into four rivers (Genesis 2:10). Here, I say that things were watered from beneath. That is an assumption made because of the fact that it had never been watered from above. We do see, however, that when the climate changed, it tells us that not only did it rain, but it also brought water from the fountains beneath (Genesis 7:11).

Let's say you have a problem believing this. Then that makes you no different from the very people who lived in that day. That period was some four to six thousand years ago. We could actually look in scripture and, by the basic timeline of men, tell how many years had passed before this change took place.

The first real climate change came to pass because of the wickedness of mankind. As a matter of fact, it had gotten to the point that only one man was seen as righteous. Again, you can read about this in God's Word. It's found in Genesis 6. What if I told you that the next real climate change would take place for the very same reason? Would you have a problem believing me? Now, men would still be just as they were in Noah's day, but the next climate change will come because God said it would. We will get to that a little later.

From the time that God revealed to Noah that a flood was coming until it actually took place was around 120 years. During that time, he built an ark as ordered by God himself. At the same time, he shared with the people the truth about what God revealed to him. The only people who believed him and began to help were his own family.

Noah preached the righteousness of God; he also preached of the judgment to come. Just as Noah believed what he preached by faith, other people would have to do the same.

We could go into all the things that went into that ark, but the point is that climate change was coming. At that time, there was absolutely no way to see it coming. If you were to believe that change was coming, you had to believe in what one man had to say about it, accept that by faith, and help build the ark for your own safety. Not one other person did that. Noah had three sons, their wives, and his wife. These were eight people, and yet, not one other person.

There's another point to be made here. Truth is truth, even if it only comes from one person. That's a hard saying. Can you imagine living in a world that has never seen rain or any precipitation fall from the sky? Day after day, everything remains the same. You get confident in all you see and all you know. All of a sudden, one man on dry land starts to build a big boat. He begins to claim that climate change is coming; he even tells you what kind of change. Would you, if you were there, believe that story?

One man, with a world of opposition, clinging to what he believed. I would like to build something here. Noah was a man known for his faith in God. The people around him had seen his life as they went about their lives, satisfying themselves with worldly pleasures. Noah was different; he walked with God. His life as a righteous man was totally different from the people around him. He wasn't a man to be deceptive or to lie. Therefore, why not believe him in this matter?

The reason is that people get so wrapped up in the things of this world, the things that they have confidence in, that they simply will not allow themselves to see anything that is not visible to the natural eye.

Now let's close this chapter with this. In about 120 years, the ark was finished. Noah, his family, and two animals of each kind, male and female, went into the ark. You can read this in Genesis 7. We see that Noah, his family, and all the animals went in, but Noah didn't shut the door. For seven days, it remained open; any man, any person, could have gone in, but no one came. The Bible says in that chapter that the Lord shut the door; now it's too late (Genesis 7:10–16). Now think about this: God's marvelous grace, his love for mankind, even though they never help build that ark at all, is still willing to leave the door open for a full seven days. Even Noah and his family would have gladly allowed any person who chose to do so. It could have been the man or woman who made fun of them the most; still, they would have been welcomed.

What a god we serve, the same God today. If you live your life selfishly, make fun of people who trust Jesus Christ, wait until you are lying on your deathbed or wait until the very last day possible to ask him to save you. He'll be there for you, and every person who is saved at that time will readily welcome you in.

For the first time ever, not only did it begin to rain, but the ground also opened up, and water came from beneath; water began to cover the earth. Climate change was beginning to happen. That change killed every living thing other than the living things on that ark. It's a sad thing to believe; one second too late. Climate change is coming again. Are you ready?

Noah preached righteousness; he also prophesied the coming event. Noah probably didn't see that as climate change, but now we know for a fact it was just that. One voice cried to the multitudes, but no one listened. From the time of that flood until the present day, it rains. Not only does it rain, but we also have other forms of water that fall from the sky, such as snow, sleet, hail, and so on, because of climate change. These things never happened before the flood. I can't even say that there were seasons; all just simply stayed the same.

There's a point I need to make before I close this chapter. The people who lived in those days before the flood, let's say, had heard of Noah and his message. In every case, he was belittled and made light of. Some of those people died before that flood happened. Wonder what happened to them as far as eternity is concerned.

Today as we watch the next climate change unfold, there's a man we speak of; his name is Jesus Christ. He is belittled and made light of; even the people who speak in his name are made fun of and belittled. We are warned of another climate change to come. It's quite possible that some or most of us will die before the next climate change occurs. If that's the case, where will you be? Noah's message was one opportunity. It was one that would have taken courage and faith to turn against all you thought you knew and all the people who opposed him.

There was an open door that any person could enter.

Jesus today is that open door of protection from the next climate change. By faith, you can step in. Just as in the days of Noah, it takes courage and faith to act on what is coming.

The first climate change forecaster not only believed what God said but also listened intensely to every word as God instructed him to move through his life. From the first time God spoke to him until climate change came, his life revolved around what he believed, and his main focus was to complete the task God had given him.

With that being said, there was no book, no science, no professor, or any other man to teach him or to point out better ways to bring things about. It was one individual, and that was the god of the universe.

Science is a great subject. As far as I know, it is an absolute in most cases, maybe all. It helps us in our everyday walk of life. But Noah had no science to guide him. He was blazing a new trail. Science cannot see the hand of God, nor can it predict the course of this world. Although man, by science, might be able to see great things and far distances, God is far beyond its reach yet just as near as a man's heart, one just like Noah's. The truth only can be seen through the eye of faith and ears that listen as the god of the universe speaks.

Look, listen, and be prepared.

Noah was the first climate change forecaster. There's a book we call the Bible that forecasts another coming climate change along with many other truths. The Bible says, "Strait is the gate, and narrow is the way, which leadeth unto life, and few there be that find it" (Matthew 7:14). You can find it. The door of the ark of Jesus Christ is still open. He, like Noah, is asking you to step in.

Then you, like Noah, can be a climate change forecaster.

CHAPTER 5

Climate Change: Is It Possible?

The Bible tells us that until the flood of Noah, it had never rained. Everything was watered from beneath the earth's surface. We also see that there were rivers, four of them (Genesis 4:10–14). It appears that these four rivers started from one and became four. We look at the word *garden* and assume it's a small place, but do we ever wonder just how big Eden was? Did it encompass the whole earth? We see where God placed an angel at the gate of Eden. The responsibility of that angel was to keep men from eating from the tree of life.

The earth was a perfect place until sin. Adam knew nothing about any kind of thorns or thistles until sin (Genesis 3:18).

We can read between chapters 3 and 6 and see all the people who were born. We can see the evil that was done on the earth that, as far as we know, was still perfect other than the sin that came out of man.

All these things we have looked at before, but I say them to build up my next point.

It appears that from the departure from the garden until Noah and the flood, which is about two thousand years past, mankind basically did as they pleased.

One point that needs to be made here is that there was no law to follow. Since I'm attempting to show climate change, I don't want to get too far off track, but there was God's consciousness and people who chose to walk with God, Noah being one of them. Man has always had that open door if they choose to follow righteousness.

But back to climate change, is it possible that when God created the earth, he set it on true north? As we live here today, the earth on an axis is set on what is called grid north. Now scientists might argue that it would be impossible for that to work. I would agree, but there is nothing impossible with God (Matthew 19:26). Is it possible that within the first two thousand years that there were scientists who truly thought that it was impossible for the earth to set and survive on anything other than true north? The same scientist might argue that no man could live for six to nine hundred years. The same scientist might say that all things would perish if it never rained.

How about a virgin woman having a baby? Is that possible? Abraham and Sarah had a son after they were a hundred years old.

The same God who enabled those things to happen can also make our little world work just as he pleases.

Just as there were spiritual and physical mindsets before the flood, we see the same thing today. Basically, the physical or worldly mindset has taken over the spiritual mindset in our world once again. We have no idea of the power of God. By faith, Noah believed it would rain when he had never seen rain; by faith, he listened to a voice from a god he had never seen; by faith, he and his family were saved from the wrath of that same Almighty God.

The men or people of that time laughed at him and mocked him. Can you imagine how stupid Noah looked to the people of that time? Well, Noah was right; it rained. More than likely, there were things that happened that he didn't expect, but it rained just as he preached for 120 years.

Again, is it possible that what we see today or what Noah had seen when the ark settled back on earth is totally different from the earth he left?

He could see the rivers, but no ocean, no lakes. Is it possible now that Noah could have seen clouds for the very first time?

Is it possible that as the water of that flood receded and began to take the form of the new earth, it formed oceans and lakes? They even froze on the north and south poles. If this happened, is that what is holding us at grid north? Now to me, it's not. It's our Almighty God that holds it where it is. But at the same time, God could use the frozen water to accomplish his will, just waiting for the right time to allow it to melt. At that time, he could put it all back underneath the earth as it was before the flood.

If it all melted, what would happen? Is there enough frozen water at each end of this earth if melted to cover this earth completely with water again? Even if it were, according to God, it will never happen by water again (Genesis 9:8–16). He would simply put it back as it was.

These are things I do not know. However, I know that things changed after the flood, even the lifespan of man. If you read the average age of people before the flood and then study the people after the flood, you can see it begins to change.

The animals also are different. (I believe.) When I say that, it means, in this case, I don't know. Animals appeared to be in complete harmony with one another before the flood, but afterward, they killed to survive. We also see that the Bible teaches that in the future, the lamb will lie down with the lion (Isaiah 11:6).

Is it possible that the way God sees this world in the present is totally different from how he viewed it in the days before the flood? Let's look at one point, for example. Noah was trying to tell the people that a flood was coming; no one listened, and no one else was even talking about it in a positive manner. Today born-again believers are looking for Jesus Christ to come and bring an end to this dispensation in which we live, being the church or grace age. We call that the rapture. Do you hear anyone talking about that event and the fact it could be close?

Is it possible that before the flood, men had gotten so confident in their own ability to create things and so self-dependent that they didn't see a need for faith in God or anything concerning him?

I can't say exactly what this earth was like before the flood. Other than that, it was different. People who study God's word understand that. They who make a choice to seek truth can see it as well. Even if I am totally wrong about true north and grid north changing by the freezing of water, a change—climate change—happened, and the people who were not prepared for that change perished.

All they had to do to be saved was to, by faith, accept what Noah preached and get on the ark. But they did nothing; therefore, they perished.

Noah and his family faced ridicule and scoffing; they were made fun of, even hated. They, by faith, faced this for 120 years. The very people who did those things to them could have walked on that ark within the last seven days before the flood and faced no scoffing at all. God's grace and his people are that way. Right up until the last second, God's grace will be there for any person who will believe.

In the last few days before God shut the door to the ark, the people of that day could see some things that could open their eyes to the fact that the time was near.

First of all, the ark was complete. Noah and his family had begun the task of getting all the animals on the ark. In the last seven days, they stayed in that ark with the door open. Any person could have seen and realized something is about to change.

Is it possible that today we can see little signs as well? Are we so busy with the cares of this life that we can't see those things? How is it different for us today from the people of that day?

Is it possible that today we have a different name for the ark of Noah? We call it the church. Day by day, that church is being built. Every day, the body of Christ is being born and placed into that building. When it is completely finished, climate change is coming.

As we move forward through this book, it's my prayer that you will see where we stand today. Is it possible that a climate change needs to occur in your heart—one that allows the Holy Spirit to cause a warming where it makes a big difference to you as an individual? The most important climate change of all starts right within the heart of man.

I realize that some of this is repetitive. The truth is that there are things we need to think about as we walk toward the future, no matter what it is.

I, as a man, have a mind that ponders how things will be at that next climate change, and I wonder about the reasons for things, just like any scientific person might. I'll have to admit I don't know. However, what if I'm right? What if this world is going back to the true north? All the scientists in this world might disagree with me just as they did with Noah. The god whom I serve can do anything he pleases, and, I might add, he does, even in spite of me. After all, he stepped out on nothing and spoke the worlds, the whole universe, into existence. Mankind is still trying to understand this one place in which we live.

So when it comes to how this world turns out after the following climate change, even if I'm wrong about the true north, I'll be perfectly content with how my god fixes things.

I completely trust his every design.

CHAPTER 6

What's Real?

From the beginning, it's been my intention to point out why climate change, or at least the first real climate change, happens. In that, I also desire to show you how God has always maintained a righteous aspect of all that has occurred through the centuries.

As we continue, I'm going to change up to some degree. I'll do my best to explain why.

Do you realize that all that has been written in this book so far is here because of my faith in the Word of God? That, to me, is real. The Bible tells us that Noah found grace in the eyes of the Lord. I found that same grace, and so have many other people over the centuries. To each of those people, just like me, that faith is real. God didn't ask me or most of the people who gained that faith to build an ark or write a book in the Bible, but at the same time, it's been the responsibility of people just like me to spread that faith to continue the spiritual line of people, which is *God within our flesh*. We place our faith in the finished work Christ did on Calvary.

From the time when Noah first stepped off the ark, it's been important for someone to continue to be a voice of God, a spokesman of the truth and what is real.

Moses, for example, didn't build an ark, but he wrote the book of Genesis and the next four books after it. There was no way that Moses met or saw any of the people we spoke of or saw any of the events.

The point is that someone had to tell him what to write. This same book that I put my faith in also tells us who that someone was. "For the prophecy came not in old time by the will of man: but holy men of God spake as they were moved by the Holy Ghost" (2 Peter 1:21).

One other thing I'd like to point out and maybe expound on both thoughts: sin did not end at the flood. Every person on the ark was sin-cursed, and sin continued on this side of the flood.

So Moses was also a sinner, just like any other man. However, God chose sinful people, people who were willing to yield their sinful bodies to do his will and to be the voice of his spirit. We will never completely overcome sin, but we can surrender our bodies to his will. All throughout scripture, we see people who willingly gave themselves to his will.

There are things in scripture, the very scripture that I've gone over, that we can say a lot more about. There are also people who write books and who do a lot more research than I have or will. As you read what I have to say about the main topic, climate change, the truth is that, actually, it's not myself whom I want you to hear.

Without even comparing myself to Moses or any other person, we all have the same goal. The desire is for you to hear the Holy Spirit as he speaks to your heart. With all that is in us, we cannot grant you what you truly need, but he can.

He can give us the truth—what we need for now and for eternity.

The history of God's Word that is behind us is real. All the things we read in scripture are real. We can stop teaching it and not talk about it, but it doesn't change a thing that happened in history, nor does it change what will happen in the future.

I want you to notice something. There are a few times that I know of in the scripture that Satan actually speaks. One of the times was when he came to Eve in the garden (Genesis 3:1–5), and the second was in the New Testament as he tempted Christ (Matthew 4:1–10). It could be more, but these two will make my point. Both times, Satan mixed the truth with a lie to make his point. He tried to make Eve question God; he tempted Christ, but Jesus used scripture to prove him otherwise. Satan also used scripture, but he used it to deceive.

Evil men want to keep people in darkness; closing your mind and heart to the past is one way to do just that. They only want you to know what they choose for you to know, not only by not allowing you to know the history but also by changing it to bring about what their desire is.

We had just seen the real climate change in the last chapter. We can go all the way through the next four thousand years or so in scripture and point out any number of things that will bring us as we travel through time to the next real climate change. My desire is to point out a few of them. However, in this chapter, we are speaking about *real*. What's *real* to you?

To Noah, no matter what the skeptics said, how much they laughed at him, time was moving toward the coming climate change, and that was real. He believed what God said and trusted only in his word, which is also real.

When we read through the chapters leading up to the flood of Noah, we see where people lived and died. Can you agree with me that the very second that those people died as individuals, each of them saw and knew the real climate change?

Looking at the history right behind each of us as individuals, we know people who have passed from this life. What kind of change did each of them see at death? Did climate change in their lives? What is one step beyond this life? There was a past behind them, and it will be some type of future after their death.

If I try to get you to focus on only what you see right around you, what have I accomplished? In reality, not a lot. But if we look at history—real history—and believe it's real, we can have a different mindset on what we need to do to prepare for our individual future. All this must be by faith in God's Word. My goal is to understand, as much as possible, biblical history. I want to see what has already come to pass and show you what is in the future through scripture; that can be eye-opening to you as an individual.

Let's look at a couple of things that were real climate change to a few people in scripture. Remember, God's domain is within your heart. His desire for you, just as he was trying to show people of the earlier times, is to change the environment and personal climate in your heart. Once that is done, what happens in this world won't matter that much because you can see your future in God.

One thing we see is when Moses went up on the mount to get the Ten Commandments (Numbers 16:30–33). Again, you can read if you wish to learn more about it. The ground opened up and swallowed about 250 men because of worshipping idols. They went about creating their own God. These were the people who should have been walking close to God. They had every reason to place their faith in him. Climate change happened right then and there, at least to those who died.

Another event we see that should have opened eyes is found in 1 Kings 18:21. Here, Elijah simply asked a question, "How long halt ye between two opinions?" Then he said, "If God be God, then follow him. If Baal be God, then follow him."

Elijah is saying, "Make up your mind."

I'll again say here as well. You can read it for yourself, but I have a few comments to make here.

My desire is to show you two events in scripture that are real climate changes on this earth, the kind that changes the whole earth as men know it. We have seen one of them being the flood. Here, I'm simply pointing out events that should have caused men to take pause and consider. More than likely, they did at the time; however, time moves forward, history is forgotten, and men turn their backs on God. Sounds familiar?

Without teaching and getting caught up in this one event, we see this; there are people who have begun to worship Baal, a false God. We see his prophets and the true prophet of God, Elijah, in this chapter. Elijah puts these prophets to the test, and they lose. After they had prayed all day and their god would not answer, they cut themselves; they tried everything they normally did, but still no answer.

Elijah had his people cover the altar with water and so on. When he prayed a simple prayer, fire came down out of heaven and consumed the altar. The god of this universe answered. Not only did the fire consume the altar, but it also consumed the false prophets. Real climate change came in an instant, at least to those false prophets.

I realize this is not the kind of climate change that we hear about today, but I'm simply showing you some significant events that have happened over the centuries. You will have to agree that it had an effect on the people involved.

These things happened between the flood and the birth, life, crucifixion, and resurrection of Jesus Christ.

What is real? Everything that I mentioned here actually happened in history. It happened to real people just like you and me.

Looking back from this point, every generation has come and gone since Adam and Eve. If we break it down to another level, every person has come and gone. That is real. Each person, whether they were a part of the story mentioned about Moses or the story about Elijah, were real people. People all the way back, even before the flood, were real people and faced real eternity.

We are surrounded by so much today that is artificial that we get it confused with reality. Men say things that they don't mean, commercials are designed to entice and will say anything to get you to buy, preachers promise false hope, and churches feed our emotions instead of our real spiritual needs. Therefore, what is real?

Deception. It's real; it is also very powerful in the days in which we live.

One of the greatest things you will ever do is to take the time to seek those things that are real. The Word of God, the Bible, is what we call it. That will reveal and always has revealed the truth. I've tried to emphasize that one thing all along, and as we go forward from this chapter, it will also be noted. It has always boiled down to an individual and God. You have to be in a position to hear his voice. I've also placed myself in the same position as any other person, as in someone whom you can listen to.

The salvation of a man's soul is real. The problem is in you knowing who has that salvation. Who can reveal the truth to you from God? The one person who you can know for sure has salvation is you. When salvation is yours, then you have an ear for truth as revealed by him, no matter who it's coming from. If I or any other person says or teaches things that are not true or partly false, the spirit that lives within you will guide you to what is true. That's when God can direct your heart, and with the possession of his spirit within you, he will reveal to you what is real and what is not.

What do you think? Do you not see just how important that one thing is to you?

Seek the truth, and find out what is real.

We have come all the way through the flood. We also have mentioned the time between the flood and Jesus Christ. As we continue, my prayer is that the Holy Spirit can use me in some small ways to open your understanding of the next coming climate change and the path we take to get to that change.

It's all in God's word waiting for you to study it out. I'm just trying to do my part to open the little window that sheds light on real climate change.

Climate change is a very spiritual matter. Allow God, through the power of his spirit in you, to come to the understanding that you need to be prepared for whatsoever comes in your physical life.

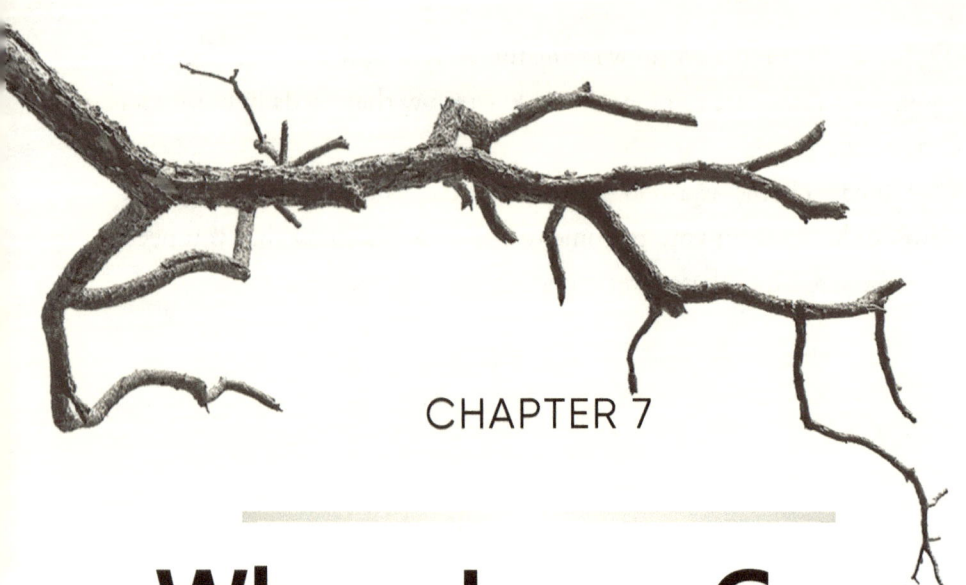

CHAPTER 7

When Jesus Gave up the Ghost

Jesus Christ was the perfect lamb of God. All the sacrifices of animals before him were mere types of his finished work on Calvary. We seldom ever think about little things in scripture. We seem to know about what we might call the important things but never look deep enough to understand the little things that really make a difference in how we gain real knowledge of God's Word.

Do you realize that every person who believed and understood that the perfect lamb was coming before Jesus Christ could not stand in the presence of God? The blood of lambs and goats could not be used as a covering for their sin; only the blood of the perfect lamb could do that (Hebrews 9:12). Therefore, all the people who died believing had to go and stay somewhere until the price was truly paid for their sin. Where was that place?

If we study, we can see. Do you remember when Jesus was on the cross? One of the thieves who was crucified with him asked to be remembered when he came unto his kingdom (Luke 23:42–43). Jesus replied, "Today thou will be with me in paradise." Well, where was *paradise*?

If we dig a little deeper, we will see.

We know that Abraham was recorded in the first book of the Bible, Genesis. But we also see him mentioned in Luke about the time of the crucifixion. Look at what it says: "And beside all this, between us and you there is a great gulf fixed: so that they which would pass from hence to you cannot; neither can they pass to us, that would come from thence" (Luke 16:26).

If you read this account, you will see two men—one rich, one poor; they both died. The rich man lifted his eyes in hell, while the poor man was found in Abraham's bosom. Evidently, they could see each other but could not cross the gulf. Jesus himself called this place paradise. All people who died believing before the death, burial, and resurrection of Jesus Christ went to this place and stayed until the perfect lamb was slain.

Now, let's look at two more verses of scripture.

"Wherefore he saith, When he ascended up on high, he led captivity captive, and gave gifts unto men. Now that he ascended, what is it but that he also descended first into the lower parts of the earth? He that descended is the same also that ascended up far above all heavens, that he might fill all things." (Ephesians 4:8–10)

"And the graves were opened; and many bodies of the saints which slept arose…" (Matthew 27:52)

You can read the following few verses there and see where they walked among men and were seen by many. That happened at the crucifixion of Jesus Christ. That is recorded history.

You have to realize that God didn't have to allow those people to be seen by the people of earth. He did that to let us know a change had happened.

Matthew 27:51, at the same time, said the earth quaked. What do you suppose that was? The Bible says in Isaiah 5:14 that hell enlarged itself. Could it be that the gulf is now gone? I don't know. That verse might be saying something completely different, but the point is that we see change.

The people who believed in the Old Testament are now able to stand in the presence of a holy and righteous God. The true lamb of God has been offered, and the blood sacrifice has been made for their sin.

Three days later, Jesus rose from the grave. There are all kinds of things to teach here, but we are working on real climate change. The climate, meaning the way that God will deal with mankind, is about to change. That change is recorded in Acts 2. There in that chapter, we see where the Holy Ghost feels on 120 believers and what we call the church was born.

If we study the scripture, it shows that this period, also called the Age of Grace, is set here to open the door of salvation to gentiles. As I say, this is a whole other study, but we must at least acknowledge it because when this age started that day in Acts, it also had an ending time. No person knows when that time will be. The church, that is, the universal church, was born on the day of Pentecost. It will run its course, and it will end. All we can do is, by understanding the trade winds of the spiritual landscape, know that the time is near. We see all kinds of signs that point us to that day; however, we do not know the day nor the hour.

These next points are something we rarely hear mentioned, but they are, however, scriptural. Since I am not truly getting into those, we won't go very deep into them, but we must understand why we see these things unfold.

God himself determined seventy weeks of desolation upon his people, the nation of Israel. We'll get back to that in a minute. The period that we are currently living in has nothing to do with those seventy weeks.

My mind is racing. How do I teach all this? My teaching ability all depends on your desire to know as you are granted by the Holy Spirit of God that either lives or desires to live within your heart.

Today, the call is to whosoever is willing to listen. Any person who sees themselves as a sinner in need of Jesus Christ can be born into God's family by faith. That is all-inclusive. Even God's chosen people can be born into God's family, the church, simply by faith.

I'm going to show you a story in scripture to make a point. It involves one man who lived during the time just before the birth of Christ (Luke 2:25). If you read a few verses here, you will see that a man named Simeon actually held Jesus as a baby. He then prays and says he is now ready for death because he has seen the Christ child, to which God had promised him.

The point is that Simeon had figured out by scripture that it was time for the Christ child to be born. He cared enough to study all that out, and God blessed him for his faithfulness.

Each of us can study the same way; we can see some things for sure, but we just can't pinpoint every event.

Now back to the seventy weeks, we see this in Daniel 9:24. Let's read it.

Seventy weeks are determined upon thy people and upon thy holy city, to finish the transgression, and to make an end of sins, and to make reconciliation for iniquity, and to bring in everlasting righteousness, and to seal up the vision and prophecy, and to anoint the most Holy.

I guess the next question would be *What is a week?* Here, one week is a period of seven years. That can be proven with a study. We also see here that you can actually tell about the time Jesus was crucified.

If you look at verse 25, it says from the going forth of the command to restore the wall, rebuild Jerusalem until the Messiah shall be seven weeks, threescore, and two weeks. That adds up to sixty-nine weeks. I can see how Simeon figured that it was time for Jesus to be born. We see now that he, being Jesus, was cut off, which basically ended the sixty-ninth week. It also ushered in the church age in which we still live today. We have no way to tell how long this age will last; only the Father knows. One day, he will tell Jesus to come get his bride, and that will end this age and the last week or the seventy weeks will begin. The last week that is spoken of in Daniel is all about God's chosen people and God's dealing with them; however, those who have not accepted Christ will be here as well.

All this can be proven in scripture, but I simply point this out to show climate change and why it's ahead of us, and it is coming. Maybe in another book, these things can be addressed. Each person should start to study and see what they can figure out. Do you realize that the Word of God is all about you as an individual? God, by the power of the Holy Spirit, wants each of us to understand, to allow him to teach and prepare us for eternity. We look at the Word of God as a book that preachers and church leaders are supposed to teach us, but that's not true. While those people might be a helpful tool, God's Word is yours and yours alone; use it for his glory.

Simeon had studied and determined that somewhere around 482 weeks had passed since the decree to rebuild the wall in Jerusalem. So, therefore, it was time for the Christ child to be born. While he was able, by study, to do just that, we, on the other hand, can see in scripture the beginning of the church, but we have no way to see the end. We could talk a little here about the things we can see that make us aware that it's closer than ever before, but the very fact that time moves forward will tell us that we must be prepared because this age will end at some point. The end of this age will be the beginning of the coming climate change.

In all this, I just wanted you to see what happened to the saints in paradise when Jesus died on Calvary. That was a changing event that we hear about somewhat, but we never hear about those people who rose on that day. What would you think the people living at that time thought when they saw those people walking around? I would say that it was talked about for some time. But we never heard about it now, although it was a very powerful event that would make people stand up and take notice.

Let's make an analogy here. We've seen the flood; only eight people on the face of this earth were saved. Now we have gone from that ark settling back to earth and mankind for the next two thousand years. Any person who believed had to do so by faith. The majority of the time between the flood and Christ was considered as being man living under the law. That was the law that God gave Moses.

To make my point, every person who believed by faith between the flood and Jesus giving up the ghost is now standing in the presence of God. They all ascended when Jesus gave up the ghost.

Now we start a *new testament*. A change has just happened. From the flood to the arrival of Christ was about two thousand years. Since Christ, it's been about two thousand years. The next significant event will be the rapture.

Therefore, we move to the next chapter.

CHAPTER 8

End of Your Time: My Time

It all ends, like it or not. Our lives are short-lived at best. Do you realize that time is nothing to God? To God, one day is like a thousand years, or a thousand years is like one day. "But, beloved, be not ignorant of this one thing, that one day is with the Lord as a thousand years, and a thousand years as one day" (2 Peter 3:8).

Just as our lives come to an end, so does each dispensation of that time. The world, as we know it, will also end.

We have come through some time in scripture. For the next few things we discuss, it's my desire to be a little more dependent on scripture because we will be talking about the next great climate change and the time leading up to that event.

I do realize, however, that for any person to believe or see any of this, that person must believe that scripture is the truth and a book to be trusted. The Bible, the Word of God, is alive. To see the things that the spirit of God desires for you to see, you must be alive in his spirit.

I place my eternal destiny in what it teaches. I love to watch as it unfolds; my desire is the same for you.

It was about two thousand years between the flood of Noah and the birth of Jesus Christ. God dealt with mankind in a few different ways during those two thousand years. Jesus was actually born during a time when God dealt with his people in the dispensation of law. As a matter of fact, the crucifixion of Jesus Christ brought an end to that dispensation. He was the fulfillment of that law (Matthew 5:17).

We will look at those things a little in the next chapter as we look at Israel's time. Israel is God's chosen people. All we see and experience is based on God's dealing with his people. It's like a big ticking clock, and we are just a part of the mechanism. We, as gentiles, should thank God for our time. That time has lasted now over two thousand years. We, the people living today, are privileged to have an opportunity to walk with Christ, even in the last days.

I feel that I must teach scripture here to bring us up to the place of the following climate change.

What changed when Jesus died on Calvary? Anything? Yes, it did. When we look at the significant events in history or scripture, sometimes we miss this one. "And, behold, the veil of the temple was rent in two from the top to the bottom" (Matthew 27:51). That is just part of that verse, but here, he's speaking of the veil that kept ordinary people, shall we say, from going into the holy of holies. Only the high priest was allowed to go behind this veil (Hebrews 9:3). Even at that, he had to have every detail covered exactly; if he failed to do so, even he would die. You can study all this if you are truly seeking to understand what events brought us to this point and are seeking to understand beyond climate change.

This veil was completely torn in two pieces, it says. You can even go back and see how this veil was made in the Old Testament (Exodus

26). We can do a lot of speculation here about many things about this veil. One of mine would be *Why does it make it so plain that it was torn in two pieces?* I'd say it represents the two testaments, one ending and another beginning, totally separate, yet both remain.

At any rate, the most important part is that because of the finished work of Christ on the cross, he being our high priest, every person who desires to can now go to the very throne of God because of his perfect blood. The perfect lamb of God being sacrificed—what a blessing!

The events recorded in this one verse says multitudes about an ending and a beginning (Matthew 27:51). We see the Old Testament saints freed, and now everyone can also talk straight to God. We no longer need someone else to do that. Jesus Christ is our high priest. Because of our relationship with him, we have access to the very throne of God. With that relationship to Christ, God's throne is never far away; as a matter of fact, his kingdom is right there within the heart of each believer. That is why we say, "We walk with him and talk with him."

Hebrews 9 perfectly describes the transition that took place when Jesus died on the cross. It tells how the high priest would go into the holy of holies once a year and offer sacrifices for the sins of the people. But Christ is that perfect sacrifice that ended all that. In essence, now God lives within the heart of each believer and will until the end of this age.

This age is your time and my time. This age is not easily seen in scripture, but it's there. If we are willing to study, we can even see the time from the death of Christ until the beginning of this age.

First, if you will take the time to study Leviticus 23 along with Matthew 26, you can see how the two chapters are relative, the point being, the Passover lamb. The disciples in Matthew prepared for that day, not realizing that Jesus would be that lamb. In Leviticus, it was a picture, a mere type; in Matthew, it was the true sacrifice.

We are looking for fifty days. In Leviticus, it was seven Sabbaths and then the next day. One Sabbath comes in this text every seven days, making a total of fifty days from Passover until Pentecost.

Jesus and his death on the cross was the true fulfillment of Passover being the perfect lamb of God.

As you read through Leviticus 23, you can see all the events carried out in the feasts they have. The Passover, the first fruits, the feast of Pentecost—those are fifty days later, that little, short period. God revealed that in scripture.

We also see the Feasts of Trumpets, which is relative to the return of Christ. It is important to understand that when we see the Feast of Trumpets as recorded in Leviticus, it's speaking of when Jesus returns to set up his kingdom on earth. The rapture is still not seen in that lineup of events. Therefore, although we can pinpoint the crucifixion and the day of Pentecost, the age in which we now live is not seen there.

Now, if you go to Acts 1:3, look at this: "To whom also he shewed himself alive after his passion by many infallible proofs, being seen of them forty days, and speaking of the things pertaining to the kingdom of God."

Notice that he was seen (forty days). In verse 4, he tells them to wait for the promise of the Father that they have heard of him.

Pentecost is fifty days, which is one of the feasts, the birth of the church.

We look back at the statement he made in Acts 1:3: "Speaking of the things pertaining to the kingdom of God."

Do you realize there is a difference between the kingdom of God and the kingdom of heaven? The kingdom of God is where God is; one of those places is in the heart of the believer. The kingdom of heaven will be established right here on earth, Jesus being the king; that's in the future after climate change.

At this moment, the kingdom of God is here on earth, but he lives in the hearts of those who are born again. His power comes from the voice of those who are willing to proclaim his truth, his gospel around this world in truth and power. He is only as strong as we allow him to be as members of his body, the church.

One day, Israel will see him in all his power and glory, right after climate change.

Let's get back to the fifty days. We can see the forty days as recorded in Acts 1:3, but we can't give a number of days until the church was born; however, we can see that it clearly says, "When the day of Pentecost was fully come." Therefore, we know that it was a ten-day period between when Jesus was taken up and when the Holy Ghost fell on the 120 believers. The disciples as well would have recognized those ten days. They understood well the day of Pentecost.

The Bible says, "Behold, now is the accepted time; behold, now is the day of salvation" (2 Corinthians 6:2).

We live in that age, a time when the Holy Spirit draws conviction in the hearts of people. When the word of God is proclaimed in truth and is heard by a sinner who is lost, that conviction becomes real. A battle begins to rage in the heart of the lost soul—a battle that can be won by the sinner simply by confessing that they are a sinner and asking Jesus Christ to be their savior. Know, by faith, that he paid the price for their sins on Calvary.

Whosoever will can become a child of God and speak directly to God by the blood of Jesus Christ.

That opportunity ends in two ways; it ends when your heart stops beating, and you draw your last breath. And if Jesus comes to receive his bride, that window of salvation is closed.

Each day that we live, and one generation gives way to another, we draw closer to that day. When scripture speaks of now and today in that verse of scripture, it means exactly that. We have no promise of tomorrow, either in our own lives or Jesus's return. There is nothing in scripture that would hinder him from returning today, right at this moment.

Jesus Christ, at the beginning of this age, was taken up, and a cloud received him out of their sight. "And when he had spoken these things, while they beheld, he was taken up; and a cloud received him out of their sight" (Acts 1:9).

I want to use that verse to make my point. It also says that while they were standing there gazing up into heaven, two men stood by and told them that Jesus would return in like manner (Acts 1:11). Here, we have to consider something. What *return* is he speaking of? Climate change will happen between these two returns of Christ.

In my opinion, it really doesn't matter which one of the two he is speaking of in this verse. The reason I say that is because the two events happened within a seven-year period. The disciples of Christ will have a part in both of them.

Let's look at the first one.

For the Lord himself shall descend from heaven with a shout, with the voice of the archangel, and with the trump of God: and the dead in Christ shall rise first: Then we which are alive and remain shall be caught up together with them in the clouds, to meet the Lord in the air: and so shall we ever be with the Lord (1 Thessalonians 4:16–17).

This is the return of Christ at the end of this age, the age we live in. The disciples whom Jesus was speaking to before he was taken up and the two men who stood by could not have known about this age at that time. It has to do with born-again believers and the body of Christ we call the church. They even could have been a part of the believers. That and how it unfolds are a whole different story, but there is a distinct difference if we study it out.

We must understand man alone cannot teach this book. Any man who attempts to teach must have the Holy Spirit of God living within him. Also, a student who desires to understand must also have that same spirit within them. No other way will work.

When Jesus returns and meets us in the air as born-again believers, at that point, the age of grace is complete. We will talk about the second return of Christ in the next chapter. It has to do with Israel's time.

What a glorious journey we are on if we only believe.

Here, let's start a new chapter.

CHAPTER 9

Israel's Time

We ended the last chapter essentially with the rapture of the church. We know, according to scripture, that only eight people were saved on Noah's ark. Though, we have no idea how many people of all nationalities and tongues will be lifted above the wrath of God when Jesus returns in the clouds. We know that there will be people of all nationalities who remain here on earth because they did not accept Christ as their lord and savior. Up until this point, things have basically remained as they were since the flood of Noah.

Every region has its traits; hot or cold; seasonal change, some years more than others. I'm sure that all this can and will be argued by someone. The truth is that ever since Noah and his generation, people have lived, and people have died. There's been good weather and bad. We've also noticed some changes in the way God dealt with people. There has always been and always will be a change of some kind, especially in the weather.

Since Noah, there have been just a few different ways God has dealt with man. However, the longest-running one was the dispensation of law. We have seen where that dispensation ended at the death, burial, and resurrection of Christ. That event ushered in the dispensation of grace. Now, because of this event (the rapture), change—even climate change—is coming once again. The time that starts right now, once Jesus has caught the church up in the clouds, has a beginning that we can see and an end that we can see in scripture. Climate change takes place within this seven-year period.

Our time began on the first day of Pentecost after the resurrection of Jesus Christ and has not ended as of yet. Today it's still a "whosoever will" salvation. Our time is what we can call it. The next period is basically for the nation of Israel, and it will last about seven years. We have mentioned that in an earlier chapter, but I'll try to be more specific here.

In Genesis 12, we see God speaking to Abram, which later became Abraham. As you read through, we can see the beginning of the nation of Israel. It would take a lot of books to uncover all that needs to be said about how this nation came to be involved in the seven-year period we are speaking of here. The truth is that their unwillingness to simply trust God and believe in the things he said created the need for disciplinary actions against them as a nation. The next climate change will put them back as God intended, so to speak.

We have seen where God determined seventy weeks of desolation upon his people. We have also seen where the sixty-nine weeks of this time ended at the death, burial, and resurrection of Jesus Christ. Now let's look at the time leading up to that last week that must take place. I'll point out that we have no way to say when this will take place other than just recognizing little things that can show us that the time is near.

Look at this verse: "And when these things begin to come to pass, then look up, and lift up your heads; for your redemption draweth nigh" (Luke 21:28). In this verse of scripture, notice one word, and let's relate it to some things—the word *redemption*. What's he saying, and to whom is he saying it?

In our time, the time of the Gentiles (Luke 21:24), it's mentioned right here in this chapter; we are redeemed by the blood of Jesus Christ. Here, Jesus is speaking to his disciples, and the redemption he's speaking of is concerning the nation of Israel. The things that are mentioned here, in most cases, will not occur until the end of our age. While we might see some of the things mentioned in verse 25, some of them will be greatly seen in the next age, the seventieth week, all concerning Israel. In this verse, we see the sun blackened and the moon turned to blood (Revelation 6:12). Therefore, we might see some things begin and maybe point us toward this time. But basically, Jesus will come for his bride, the church, like a thief in the night when we least expect it, and then these things will begin.

Let's take the time here to try and understand why these events have and will come to pass. Jesus spoke a lot in parables. Look at what he said in Luke 14:16. Without writing the scripture, I'll just explain the content, and you can read it.

He tells a parable about a man that prepares a great supper and bids his friends, family, and neighbors to come and eat. None of them come. Therefore, he turns to the poor and the lame and instructs his servant to go into the hedges and highways and get whosoever will to come and eat.

Jesus came to the nation of Israel first. He was rejected by them; therefore, he bid anyone who would come. Even in the first nine chapters of Acts, right after the church was formed, the focus was on the nation of Israel. It was offered to the Jews first, and they still, as a nation, rejected God's hand. In Acts 9, we see the salvation of a man called Saul, who later became the apostle Paul, the apostle to the Gentiles.

"Then Paul and Barnabas waxed bold, and said, It was necessary that the word of God should first have been spoken to you: but seeing ye put it from you, and judge yourselves unworthy of everlasting life, lo, we turn to the Gentiles." (Acts 13:46)

The apostle Paul wrote most of the epistles in the New Testament. It was he whom God gave the responsibility to lay the foundation of the newly born church.

"If ye have heard of the dispensation of the grace of God which is given me to you-ward" (Ephesians 3:2). You can read more about it in this chapter.

Although the apostle Paul was the apostle to the Gentiles, he, as a Jew, still loved his people and was very concerned about their eternal souls. His desire was to see them saved. I want to show you something in Romans that I believe shows the real heart of the apostle Paul. This is something that I see here; you might see it differently, but it's worth the time to study.

In the book of Romans, the apostle is teaching Roman people who are Gentiles. If you take the time to read Romans 8, the last part of that chapter, it shows us, as Gentiles, just how secure we are in the love of Christ. Now it appears that chapter 12 should be the next chapter after chapter 8 the way he starts it off. Romans 12 starts off with, "I beseech you therefore, brethren." If you read the last verse in Romans 8, you will see why I say they tie together.

In chapters 9, 10, and 11, his whole mindset changes to the nation of Israel, his people. Look at what he says in Romans 9:1–3: "I say the truth in Christ, I lie not, my conscience also bearing me witness in the Holy Ghost, That I have great heaviness and continual sorrow in my heart. For I could wish that myself were accursed from Christ for my brethren, my kinsmen according to the flesh."

The apostle Paul is saying that if he could and salvation would come to his brethren, he himself would go to hell and be separated from Christ. Chapters 9, 10, and 11 are all about Israel and how they are set aside for a while and that we are drafted in by adoption.

You can read all three chapters, but I just want to show you a verse, maybe two, in chapter 11.

For I would not, brethren, have you ignorant of this mystery, lest ye be wise in your own conceits, that a hardening in part has befallen Israel, until the fullness of the Gentiles be Come in; and so all Israel shall be saved: even as it is written, There shall come out of Zion the Deliverer; He shall turn away ungodlinesses from Jacob: And this is the covenant from Me unto them, When I shall take away their sins.

The apostle Paul is showing us how the nation of Israel is being set aside for a while. When the time of the Gentiles is complete, the seventieth week for Israel will begin.

My desire is to show you the next climate change. In doing that, I feel that I must lay the foundation for that change. Therefore, I need to try and establish the basic difference between the nation of Israel, the way and the reason God deals with them, and we, the people, the Gentiles living in this age. In 1 Thessalonians 5:2, it says this: "For yourselves know perfectly that the day of the Lord so cometh as a thief in the night."

This verse is speaking of when Jesus comes for his bride. We could call that the first event on the day of the Lord. When he returns to redeem Israel, it will be in power and not so much like a thief.

However both are closely related, but there is a distinct difference between the two events. If I were to teach all that unfolds at this time, it would take another book or more. Just consider, in Luke 21, where we noted that it is similar to Matthew 24, the disciples Jesus is speaking to will be a part of both events because they believe and trust in him.

Jesus will establish his kingdom, the kingdom in which he is the rightful king, the king of Israel as it should have been, right here on this earth at the end of the seventieth week. His disciples will be a part of that kingdom (Matthew 19:28). I feel a need here to make another point about this last seven-year period that basically concerns Israel.

God created a place called hell for the devil and his angels (Matthew 25:41). However, any person who rejects Christ will end up in that place as well. We also see that in that verse. It's the same way with the seventieth week. Every person who has trusted Christ by faith will be lifted above all that happens in that period. Those who rejected the call by faith to salvation will be on this earth during that climate change.

I often make the point that God has chosen to use sinful people to do his will upon this earth—people who are willing to forget themself and allow the spirit of God to direct their path and yield their sin-cursed bodies to his leadership.

Satan also needs a human body to have his will done. What we don't realize is that there is no middle ground. We are either allowing ourselves to be used by one power or the other. "He that is not with me is against me; and he that gathereth not with me scattereth abroad" (Matthew 12:30).

I pointed out that the disciples of Jesus Christ would be part of both events of the coming of Christ. The rapture of the church and the return in his glory as the king of the Jews. Many or most of the Jews of that day denied Christ, but these men gathered with him. Other women and men gathered with him, but Israel as a nation rejected him as their savior or king. Over the last two thousand years or so, there have been many Jews who have acknowledged that Jesus is the savior of the whole world and the king of the Jews; however, as a nation, Israel still rejects him as both.

Therefore, that seventieth week will come. It is Israel's time, a time when God will finish the desolation he promised upon that nation for their disobedience, a time when the second climate change will take place. Now let's see what it will be like during that time.

CHAPTER 10

When God the Father Promises

I'll start this chapter with a verse of scripture.

Knowing this first, that there shall come in the last days scoffers, walking after their own lust, And saying, where is the promise of his coming? for since the fathers fell asleep all things continue as they were from the beginning of the creation. (2 Peter 3:3–4)

In this verse, we see that a promise was made of Christ's return. Men scoff at that promise and make little of it. I believe I have already made a point that I am about to make again. Whether you or I believe anything about God's plan or wonder whether he will keep his promises or not will never change one thing.

Man today might refuse to speak of God's word, even try and change it, but all that we see and hear will never change one little part of what God is doing. Let's look at another verse: "For verily I say unto you, Till heaven and earth pass, one jot or one tittle shall in no wise pass from the law, till all be fulfilled" (Matthew 5:18).

When you get to the place where you feel you cannot depend on anyone to be faithful or keep their promises, you can always depend on God to keep his.

The Bible teaches us that many false prophets will come and say many things. However, when a prophet of God speaks, it will come to pass. For instance, God spoke to Noah and told him to prepare for a flood. Noah proclaimed or prophesied what God said as he prepared as God told him to. He was a true prophet. God speaks to men who are prophets and reveals things to them that he wants us to know. The knowledge comes straight from God—knowledge that is unknown until it is revealed by God's prophet.

The knowledge that I reveal comes from God's word. For some two thousand years, God has spoken to men through his Word. I will say that it still takes the Holy Spirit to reveal that knowledge, but there is a distinct difference. People like me still have a heartfelt desire to reveal the promises of God. But the way God reveals his will to man today is not at all the same.

God's promises are still real, no matter how hard man tries to hide them from us. Real climate change is a promise that is prophesied in scripture. Mankind must prepare for what is in front of us. Every person must stand before God; that also is a promise of God. You and I might not live to see climate change that will happen, but if not, that promise of God will be kept without any doubt. If you remember, God determined seventy weeks of desolation on his people in Israel. Sixty-nine weeks have been accomplished; the promise was for seventy. God hasn't forgotten that last week.

Our world today has forgotten the promises of God, good and bad. Time passes; one generation gives way to another without much change, although we continue to slide down, or worse, fall off a spiritual cliff by our own actions. Since, seemingly, God the Father does nothing about it, we assume our lifestyles are well within his tolerance or guidelines.

Be not deceived. God sees and records what he sees, and his promises are still intact.

There's a story found in scripture that might fit well here. In 1 Kings 21 and 2 Kings 9, King Ahab wanted a vineyard that Naboth owned. His wife Jezebel had him killed so that Ahab could have the vineyard. God instructed his prophet Elijah to tell them that the dogs would lick their blood at the same place where Naboth died. Ahab repented, so therefore, God instructed Elijah to tell Ahab that his children would be punished in his stead. In other words, he was spared, but his son faced punishment because of his actions. Jezebel, Ahab's wife, was also told that the dogs would lick her blood at this same place.

These people took the belongings of a man who was simply seeking to obey God. They wanted it for selfish reasons and could care less about what God thought.

Now let's see what happened next. If you read in 2 Kings 9, you will see that God kept his promise. Ahab's son was shot with an arrow, and Jezebel fell from a window, and the dogs ate her just as God had said. I'm sure that Jezebel, knowing what had been prophesied, thought that after all the years had passed, God had forgotten, but God neither slumbers nor sleeps. His prophecies are real and will always come to pass.

Again, another book could be written about this one event. My prayer is that each person who reads what is said in this book will take the time to study God's Word and grow in his grace.

For the people of our generation to think that things will always stay as they are, to think that just because we put God and his Word out of our minds and act like he doesn't exist, makes us have this same mindset as those people did.

God promised a flood, and it came. He also promised that this world would see destruction again, and it will just as he promised. Only this time, it will be by fire. Don't be deceived by the things you hear and see around you today. Begin to seek God and his will. One day, you will be glad you did.

Jesus promised his disciples in John 14 that he would come again. He said he was going to prepare a place for us. He said, "If I go away, I will come again and receive you unto myself."

He will keep that promise just as he has every other promise he has ever made. He also said, "If you have seen me, then you have seen the Father." He, Jesus, is God in flesh (John 14:7). This book is about true climate change. The world speaks of it as if God has nothing to do with it. Men of this world are telling us what will happen in the future if we don't change. Just like the false prophets spoken of in scripture, there is some truth to what they say. The problem is that there is nothing physical about ourselves that we can change to stop God's climate change. What we need to change is spiritual, not to stop climate change but to be prepared.

That promise is coming. It is a promise he made to all of us. In a significant way, it is a warning to every living soul to get right with him because of that very fact.

God promised, and he is not slack concerning his promises as some men count slackness. The Bible tells us that, in 2 Peter 3:9, he is long-suffering, not willing that any should perish.

Fathers in the flesh make promises to their children and other people that they don't keep. God will keep his. One of the very reasons we are where we are in our world today is because of the slackness in which men keep their promises. That being said, make no mistake; it did not catch God by surprise. He knew from the beginning just how men would be.

Before I leave this chapter on the promises of God and move on toward the actual coming climate change, let me show you something in the first part of Revelation. This book is the last book in the Bible. Since the last *Amen* was written in this book, nothing has been added to the scripture. Men have tried to disown it, destroy it, change its wording, and keep mankind from reading it. However, its true form is still as powerful today as it ever was.

In the first part of this book, we see a picture of the church, the very church that Jesus, God in flesh, died and rose again for.

In the Old Testament, at one point, Elijah, the prophet of God, was discouraged. Look at what God told him: "Yet I have left me seven thousand in Israel, all the knees which have not bowed unto Baal, and every mouth which hath not kissed him" (1 Kings 19:18).

In the Revelation, as we see the church unfold in the first three chapters, we see the same weakening of the influence thereof.

While the church in its prime was a very powerful voice for the voice of God, it has been weakened by the powers to be. At the same time, just as God told Elijah in the Old Testament that he had people who had not bowed to Baal, he still has people who stand for his righteousness today. Those of that mindset will be here all the way up until the rapture of the church.

In this weakening of the voice of God in our church setting, we can see the day of real climate change as that day approaches. It's part of the landscape just before real climate change happens.

As you read this book, let's assume you are a church member. As you go to church this week, you expect to see your pastor stand behind the pulpit as usual. As you sit in your usual spot and go through the normal Sunday routine, and it becomes time for your pastor to speak, another man stands in his place. This is how he starts his message to you: "And I, brethren, could not speak unto you as unto spiritual, but as unto carnal, even as unto babes in Christ. I have fed you with milk, and not with meat: for hitherto ye were not able to bear it, neither yet now are ye able."

This is what the apostle Paul said to the church at Corinth in chapter three.

Is that where we are now—churches full of babies that can't handle the meat that scripture offers? There are seven churches mentioned in the first three chapters of the Revelation. Of these seven churches, God says he is somewhat against all but two of those churches.

I only point this out to say that as we watch the church age unfolds, we can see the coming era of climate change as we watch the church becoming less and less the vessel that God ordained her to be. Over the last two thousand years or so, some part of every generation can be seen in the things mentioned in every church in this lineup. However, if you notice, the last church mentioned "Laodicea," God says about this church, "You are neither cold nor hot. How I wish you were one or the other. So because you are lukewarm—neither hot nor cold—I am about to spit you out of My mouth!"

I realize that's not word for word, but you get the point. If you continue to read, God says that they think they are rich and in need of nothing, but as God sees them, they are wretched and blind and poor.

I'd say, in my opinion, this is where our churches are today. You have an opinion, just like I do. Just as I can look and watch, and decide for myself where we are as a people, so can you. Remember, these are individuals that God deals with.

While he will deal with the angels at each of these churches mentioned, which are the pastors or those in leadership roles, that is totally beside the point as far as you, as an individual, prepare to stand before him.

Leaders will be held accountable for their shortcomings in listening to the spirit of God; however, that will not affect how he deals with you. How you stand before God is totally your responsibility.

As we see our churches become more about mankind and less about the spiritual aspect of their lives, then we know that what I am calling—climate change is near. People are born as babies; they mature and become mature adults with the ability to eat real food and forget the baby food they once depended on.

The church was born one day; we talked about that. It matured and, at one point, for many years, prospered as a valid source of spiritual power, seeing salvation come to multitudes of people. Today, as we watch it become (lukewarm) and once again, just like an old man in his second childhood, it depends on baby food and not real spiritual meat to keep it going.

The most significant problem with this is that the mindset of the average church is one of (great spiritual revival). Remember the verse that said they were blind, wretched, and poor? It's never been what man thinks of any church but rather what Jesus Christ thinks that truly matters. We can say that we have a great church, but if the true power of God is not there, then it is poor, wretched, and blind, no matter what we say about it.

Basically, in every church, in every denomination, there are born-again believers. Some of them are even in leadership roles and can see what is happening to the church, the body of Christ. They are even scoffed at and belittled if they try to point out the truth in some cases.

Satan intervenes in anything that is godly. It's no different now from when it was just before the crucifixion of Christ. Now that we are some two thousand years past that time, let's look and see. John 18:39 tells us that the Jews had a custom. At Passover, they would release a prisoner. Pilate reminded them of this and asked them whom he should release, Jesus the "King of the Jews" or Barabbas? They chose to crucify Jesus and to set free a known criminal. If you read this same account in Matthew 27, take special notice of verse 25: "Then answered all the people, and said, His blood be on us, and on our children." That was what the Jews said about Jesus.

I simply point that out in hindsight to ask this question: Do you think they made the right choice?

We, in our world, also have choices to make. We live in a time when the gospel and Jesus Christ are evil spoken of. That is even true, in some cases, in most of our churches. When I say "evil spoken of," you must realize in what context I'm making that remark. To keep it simple, is the Jesus Christ preached in your church today the same one they preached about some fifty years ago? If you are not that old, be vigilant; it's your eternity we are speaking of.

We could go on and on, but the bottom line is climate change is unfolding, and if we look closely, we can see it. Whether you and I live to see it or not, it still has all to do with the nation of Israel and the church. Of these two entities, how God deals with them won't change. Only you can prepare yourself for how he deals with you.

In this age (the church age), God promised that through and by the very blood of Jesus, his only begotten son, your sins could be covered simply by believing and trusting his finished work on Calvary. By faith in him, we, who believe, will have eternal life and be above the coming climate change as it comes. Just like all the other promises of God, you can depend on this one as well.

Again, there are books written on what it means to be born again and how it takes place. Your true relationship with Jesus Christ is within your own heart, personally between you and him. Don't allow me as I write or any other man to decide that promise for you. You yourself should make your calling and election sure. "Wherefore the rather, brethren, give diligence to make your calling and election sure: for if ye do these things, ye shall never fall" (2 Peter 1:10).

If you study the nine verses before this one, you can see what he is saying. Notice that in verse 4, he says this: "Whereby are given unto us exceeding great and precious promises." I'd like to make a statement here that I think is valid. You will have to decide for yourself what you might think.

If I, or any person, give you a one-million-dollar gift, what you do with that gift is up to you. The gift of salvation is free. Jesus Christ loved you so much. He died and rose again to purchase that gift for you.

Just like the one-million-dollar gift, what you do with the free gift of salvation is up to you. For those who have received the gift of salvation, there is a judgment seat where we stand before Christ to receive crowns for what we choose to do with the gift of salvation, all in God's word.

Having a pastor in the church you attend is an absolute blessing to point all these out for your spiritual education. However, that is not promised to believers; therefore, just as an individual might waste a whole gift of a million dollars, the gift of salvation is yours to decide.

Use the gift that is presented to you wisely. While the gift of salvation is free, the things you can receive from that gift have to be earned. All is a promise of God the Father.

CHAPTER 11

Climate Change: The Church Is Gone

We start this chapter with the rapture, or the taking away of the church. There's a lot we could say about this, but let's just ask a question: Can you even imagine living in a world that is basically destitute of all righteousness, a world where evil has complete control of? You might think or say that we are already there; sometimes it seems that way, but God's people, those who have his spirit, still hold back the forces of complete evil, believe it or not. We see this in 2 Thessalonians 2:7: "For the mystery of iniquity doth already work: only he who now letteth will let, until he be taken out of the way."

The next verse says that the wicked one shall be revealed. While the church and God's spirit is still here, there is a battle that rages in the hearts of most people. Once that opposing power is gone, there will be no real resistance against evil. At that time, you will be able to see the wicked one.

We have mentioned some things that are seen in the first three chapters of the Revelation. As we move to this chapter, if you'll notice, the writer, John the Beloved, says he sees something. "After this I looked, and behold, a door standing open in heaven" (Revelation 4:1). The church has just been taken away. You will not see the church mentioned again until Revelation 19. We could say more about that, but climate change is our target, so let's see what happens starting after Revelation 4.

As we watch some of this unfold, remember in Noah's day, every person who was not on the ark perished. When this world is destroyed by fire, all men will not die; many will, but not all. Jesus Christ will establish his kingdom right here on this earth. It will be a new heaven and a new earth, but it will still be here.

At this time, in this chapter, let's find the middle of the next seven years that we will see. Remember, this is the last week spoken of by the prophet Daniel. The word of God even tells us that unless these days be shortened, no man would live; it is absolutely that destructive. "And except those days should be shortened, there should no flesh be saved: but for the elect's sake those days shall be shortened" (Matthew 24:22).

God's purpose in this period is not to destroy all flesh but to finish his promise to his people in Israel. However, the world, as we know it, will be changed. So let's find the middle to make some very significant points.

We'll start in Revelation 13:5: "And there was given unto him a mouth speaking great things and blasphemies, and power was given unto him to continue forty and two months."

As I get into this, I'll be the first to admit—I cannot explain it all. Like a lot of other people, I am still studying and trying to understand.

It's just simply a passion. My desire is to create that same desire in each person who reads.

I, however, understand that forty-two months is exactly half of a seven-year period. When John the Beloved sees this beast, as he calls it, rise out of the sea, one-half of the seven-year period has already taken place.

Do you remember reading in the first few chapters of this book that when Adam and Eve left the Garden of Eden, all things seemed to be just as they were for a while? Well, during the seven-year tribulation period, it's the same way; the world will think they have basically defeated God and all his people, and now they can do as they please.

One thing that always amazes me about people is that they never realize that they, or any of us, don't live on this earth forever. We all die. If you have the privilege to do as you please, how long will that last?

God and Satan are opposites. While God's whole and only desire is for you and me to know the absolute truth, Satan's desire is now and always has been to deceive. In the first forty-two months, God cannot be found on this earth; Satan has complete power to deceive, and that is exactly what he does.

Let me give you an example of the difference between how God in the body of Jesus Christ might say something and how Satan might cause the world to look at the same thing.

This is what Jesus said in Luke 12:51: "Suppose ye that I have come to give peace on earth? I tell you, nay, but rather division."

Now look at this: "For when they shall say, Peace and safety; then sudden destruction cometh upon them, as travail upon a woman with child; and they shall not escape (1 Thessalonians 5:3).

As Jesus sees things, it's not about having peace but glorifying the Father with your life, and that in itself is bringing about division in this world. As Satan and the world sees it, it has nothing to do with God and glorifying him but self-pleasure and self-gratification.

Mankind is looking today for peace here on earth, and without God, they will accept any person whom they think can bring that peace. The only real peace is in the knowledge of Christ. He and only he can bring true peace. The peace that man in their flesh desires is the kind that allows them to do and act as they please.

What if what you desire actually brings no peace to someone else? Can we call that real peace? I also realize that what pleases God is not pleasing to the world. But we still have to understand that this world belongs to our god, and therefore, he has the authority to do with it as he pleases, and mankind cannot design it as he pleases and make it last at any rate.

We talked about Revelation 4 and the catching up of the church. Now comes real climate change. In the following few chapters of the Revelation, we see the church in heaven looking down upon this earth as climate change is beginning to take place.

Remember the forty-two months? Well, bad things are beginning to happen. The spirit of God, as we now know it, left with the rapture of the church. However, God's grace is still around, and although the gospel might be a little different, people can still make a choice to yield to God's spirit and denounce Satan. But for how long?

In Revelation 11:3, we see two witnesses. They prophesize 1,203 score days. If you figure that out, it's about forty-two months or three and one-half years. No one can do anything to hurt these witnesses until an appointed time, and then they are killed.

As we watch this period when this world goes through real climate change, once again, you, my friend, don't want to be on this earth.

I say that here because, in reality, these two witnesses are trying to help the people of this earth, even in a terrible time. They are hated and despised because of who they represent. Remember, the Holy Spirit is not here now to speak to man's heart. If any person turns toward God, it's all on their own. We can already see that to some degree today.

The nation of Israel and those who believe in the death, burial, and resurrection of Jesus Christ are hated, even today.

Now let's look a little deeper in this chapter, Revelation 11. These are the witnesses of God Almighty. They have great powers to do great things. You can read about them in this chapter. In verse 7, we see where a beast rises out of the bottomless pit, makes war with them, and kills them. As you continue to read, their bodies are left out and not buried. They lie there for three and a half days, and God raises them from the dead. During the time they are left lying in the street, people rejoice and send gifts, all because these two prophets are dead.

Although these two prophets have the power to hurt and cause bad things to happen, they still represent a glorious god. This god is rejected by the world. Even in the face of terrible things happening, he is still rejected by the masses.

As things continue to get worse, let's look at another attempt by God, even after the church is gone, to open the eyes of the deceived.

And I saw another angel fly in the midst of heaven, having the everlasting gospel to preach unto them that dwell on the earth, and to every nation, and kindred, and tongue, and people, Saying with a loud voice, Fear God, and give glory to him, for the hour of his judgement is come; and worship him that made heaven and earth, and the sea, and the fountains of waters. (Revelation 14:6–7)

This will be the last attempt to cause people to turn toward God. We mentioned before that it's not God's will that any should perish, but all should come to repentance. I realize that. At present, people are born into the family of God; we are part of the bride of Christ—that is, the true church. However, people who turn to him after the church is gone will have a different relationship with him. In the church age, the gospel of grace is preached, but we see a change here. It is called the everlasting gospel.

Climate change is the judgment of God. It was the first time, and it will be again. We are in a time just before it comes. There's one more thing we need to see and realize about the Revelation. The very fact that it is written lets us know that all things that are going on can't be written all at the same time. If we were to give an example, it's you or me writing about a burning house or an automobile accident. So many things happen at the same time that there is no way to put it all in one sentence or paragraph. Therefore, you simply write all that you see as you remember it unfolding. We might look at it as confusing, but the truth is that all of it is God's judgment, and you don't want to be a part of it.

Another way to look at it with more clarity is this: if you were standing on the edge of a cliff, knowing you could jump and probably not be killed but were not sure how much you would be hurt, would you jump?

At this moment in this book, we are looking into the future. The possibility of knowing Jesus Christ and avoiding this period is still here. One day, it will not be here; therefore, prepare to meet him now.

Speaking of that, we are still looking at the first half of this period. We will see in a little while that there are people who do listen to the everlasting gospel and turn to God. The question is if you were there, would you be one of them?

Let's look at this from God's perspective. God sent his only begotten son, who was born of a virgin, lived, and suffered more than any other man according to scripture, went to the cross of Calvary, was crucified, and then rose from the grave, all because he loved you and me. All he asks is that we, by faith, accept that sacrifice, and salvation is freely yours and mine.

Therefore, if you, I, or any person understands that but rejects God's call to salvation, what will happen to that person once the door of the church is closed because of the rapture?

Look at this verse: "And for this cause God shall send them strong delusion, that they should believe a lie" (2 Thessalonians 2:11).

We are looking at this from God's perspective. The age to which we are presently living is not playtime. As citizens of the world, we think very little about the severity of circumstances once we die or if this age comes to a close. Your salvation to God the Father is a serious business. Believe it or not, it's also a serious business to Satan. That's why he does all he can now to deceive, lie, and even enter our church and cause falsehood. He knows that if he can keep you and me from accepting Christ in our lifetime or in this age, he wins, at least as far as an individual's soul is concerned.

God says that he himself will cause you to be deceived by the lies of the Antichrist during this period. There will be people who are saved, though. We see them in this verse: "And when he had opened the fifth seal, I saw under the altar the souls of them that were slain for the word of God, and for the testimony for which they held" (Revelation 6:9).

There is more to be read here about those souls and how long they will be there. We also can see that more will be saved, but when they acknowledge the existence of God, they die for their stand for him.

The last thing I will point out in this chapter is that somewhere along the end of this forty-two-month time frame, Satan will sit where he should not, declare he is God, and demand to be worshipped. "But when you shall see the abomination of desolation, spoken of by Daniel the prophet, standing where it ought not, (let him that reads understand,) then let them that be in Judaea flee to the mountains" (Mark 13:14).

Now we'll tie this verse to Revelation 13:8: "And all that dwell upon the earth shall worship him, whose names are not written in the book of life of the Lamb slain from the foundation of the world."

It's a lot to be said about all the Revelation, and I love seeking to understand it all, but my desire is for you who reads to know and understand that another true climate change is coming. If you continue to read this chapter, you will see that there will be a number given, basically 666. If you do not receive this number, you will not be able to buy or sell. If you do take it, you will seal your own doom.

Although we can see a lot of bad things that have happened up until this chapter and, as stated before, it's in the writing of a book, and it's hard to tell how it all unfolds, it's all bad, and you don't want to be here during this time.

We, as a people, the citizens of the world, have a problem giving and receiving discipline today. This has brought about an attitude that most people have, shall we say, no punishment, at least not long term. We can do almost anything and get by with it. Parents, teachers, and law enforcement officers all have to be very careful about how they handle themselves because of the threat of judgment upon them for attempting to do right. Even our churches, the membership thereof, caution their pastors with dismissal if any type of disciplinary preaching is done.

We see here after the church is gone, that is the true church. There will be churches and people that represent religion during this time; however, what we are seeing is a far cry from a lack of discipline. Now you will be killed for acknowledging the true God.

In our lives today, if we think we are getting by with our sinful lives we are deceived, we are not. Today good is evil spoken of. As we progress toward the day when the church is actually gone, that will get worse. In the first forty-two months after, when Satan has his way, evil will rule completely.

As we finish, please understand something. Everything you see is a spiritual battle. It starts in the heart of every man. Because of whom victory is given there, nations, countries, and, yes, even cities and villages are governed. They yield themselves to serve either the god of glory or Satan. But be not deceived by what you see. God has already won the battle. As we watch the spiritual battle of this world unfold, it's all about you and whom you will choose to rule your life. We look and see a lot of people, millions of them. We listen to a lot of talks, religion, politics, and even just discussions around the table or water fountain. At all this, it still boils down to what you know to be the truth, the truth between you and the true god of the universe.

I've often stated that in every good deed that is done, Jesus shed his blood and gave his all for the goodness that flows out of people. On the other hand, all the evil deeds that have ever been done and ever will be done didn't cost Satan one dime; he gets it all for nothing.

Here in Revelation 13, he seems to have won; evil seems to be prevailing. If you are a part of it here, you might even think you are victorious. In the next few chapters, God, the god of the universe, will speak. Climate change is here.

We spoke of Israel's time. Well, this is it. They are the people who are spoken of in the verse we mentioned. "For the elect's sake, the days will be shortened." This time, what we see in the Revelation is comparable to the flood of Noah. The difference is it's not water this time; it's hellfire and brimstone.

Just as the people of Noah's day doubted, there will be people who will doubt this time. They will doubt and continue to live their sin-cursed lives right up until the hellfire and brimstone start, and then just as in Noah's day, it will be too late.

Climate change is real. It has nothing to do with small physical changes we see in our weather patterns as a rule but all to do with the spiritual battles in the lives of Israel and mankind in general.

A number of things could be said and taught about the events that transpire in the Revelation, far too many to mention in one book. Make it your purpose in the life you have left to know all about the climate change that God will pass upon this earth. You will be glad that one day, you did.

CHAPTER 12

King of Kings, Lord of Lords

In the beginning, God created the heaven and the earth (Genesis 1:1). This is the very first verse in the Bible. There's another verse that says this: "But without faith it is impossible to please him: for he that cometh to God must believe that he is, and that he is a rewarder of them that diligently seek him" (Hebrews 11:6).

The same god who stepped out on nothing and spoke the universe into existence will still be speaking in the last part of the Revelation. The same god who gives life can also end it as we know it. Those who, over the centuries, placed their faith in him and diligently sought him will be watching in a secure place as the last part of everything that must transpire takes place. Climate change is in its last phase. The armies of this world are set to battle for the existence of things as they are, but to no avail.

At this point in the book of Revelation, we are seeking a new heaven and a new earth. "And I saw a new heaven and a new earth: for the first heaven and the first earth were passed away; and there was no more sea" (Revelation 21:1).

Let's look at one other verse that needs to be mentioned here: "But thou, O Daniel, shut up the words, and seal the book, even to the time of the end; many shall run to and fro, and knowledge shall be increased" (Daniel 12:4).

What we are about to see, and has already started in the Revelation, is the reopening of the book that Daniel sealed. The prophet Daniel and the apostle Paul were both shown things that they were not permitted to say. We see this from the apostle Paul in 2 Corinthians 12:4: "How that he was caught up into paradise, and heard unspeakable words, which is not lawful for a man to utter."

Daniel was a little different, though; he didn't understand it all but had the desire to know. Those things he desired to know are revealed in the Revelation.

Just consider all the people who go to and fro, most of whom are so wrapped up with their own selves, they never even consider the hand of God. They simply assume all things will continue as they are, or their trust is in man's ability to protect them.

There's a saying that uses the letters that it takes to spell *Bible*. We can call it an acronym. "Basic Instructions Before Leaving Earth."

That's what the word of God is, an instruction book. In its pages, all you need to be prepared for eternity can be found.

The people who are here at this point in the Revelation will truly long for a time when they could find those instructions, but now it's far too late.

Jesus said in Matthew 6:25, "Is not life more than meat to eat, or raiment for the body?"

We could go on and on. *Prepare to meet thy God.* That is the essence of all that we can say. Facing him unprepared is an awful thing.

Therefore, let's look at this time of true climate change. We'll use scripture and allow that to speak for us.

First of all, who is, and always has been, the King of kings and Lord of lords? It's the god of the universe. We know him in the flesh as Jesus Christ. The truth is that simple, and the problem is that the people of this world will not recognize him as that, which is his rightful position.

The Jews didn't see him as their king, and the rest of the world will not allow him to be their lord.

With that statement made, I realize that there are many Jews who see him as king and lord just as there are many other people that see him as lord.

If you remember, the King of kings and Lord of lords was beaten. A crown of thorns was placed on his head, and then he was crucified. This happened some two thousand years ago. When he returns to this earth as the King of kings and Lord of lords, those wounds that were put on him by his people will still be visible. The very people who are saved from destruction at the end of this seven-year period when he becomes their king, the king of this earth, will ask him, "What are these wounds in thine hands? Then he shall answer, Those with which I was wounded in the house of my friends" (Zechariah 13.6).

If you read a few more verses, you will see that two-thirds of the people will die, but one-third will be refined as gold and silver. That is the prophecy of this period that we are seeing here.

You can compare Zechariah 13 and 14 with Revelation 19. Zechariah simply prophesied the events that take place in Revelation. Although we don't see it recorded in Revelations, it is prophesied in Zechariah that Jesus will stand on the Mount of Olives. The mountains will part unto a great valley according to what Zechariah prophesied. The King of kings will destroy the enemies of Israel with the word of his mouth.

There are two things I want you to see here. The first in Revelation 19:17–18:

And I saw an angel standing in the sun; and he cried with a loud voice, saying to all the fowls that fly in the middle of heaven, Come and gather yourselves together to the supper of the great God; that you may eat the flesh of kings, and the flesh of captains, and the flesh of mighty men, and the flesh of horses, and of them that sit on them, and the flesh of all men, both free and bond, both small and great.

Now Revelation 14:20:

And the winepress was trodden without the city, and blood came out of the winepress, even unto the horse bridles, by the space of a thousand and six hundred furlongs.

This is all part of Armageddon; it's a real place and a place you want no part of.

When we read *one thousand and six hundred furlongs*, just how long is that? That, my friend, is a space of two hundred miles. It is filled with blood so deep it would touch a horse's bridle. One furlong is 660 feet. And it says it's one thousand and six hundred furlongs.

Jesus is going to be the king of this earth one day in the future. Israel is going to go through that last week that God promised them as prophesied by Daniel.

Mankind has a tendency to forget. Just as the people ask Jesus where his wounds come from because they were not taught the truth. We all put those things out of our minds.

We might look at the flood of Noah and feel that it was a very hard thing. The next climate change will be very unforgiving and unforgettable.

I pointed out that Jesus, when he returns as the King of kings, will stand on the Mount of Olives because when he comes some seven years earlier for the church, it will be in the clouds. He'll not touch the earth. But when he returns in all his glory to establish his kingdom here, it will be forever. This time, he will be received as the king of Israel, and the nation of Israel will inherit this whole earth.

This is real climate change, and It's somewhere in our future. Whether this generation lives to see it or not, it will happen.

Every generation has an opportunity to prepare for it. The people responsible for teaching it today very seldom speak of it, but it will happen nonetheless. If you, as an individual, are not aware of the truth and how it all unfolds, then consider your options. Although God will judge the unfaithfulness of those who should prepare you, which will be to their demise, that won't take away from your duty to know the truth.

Seek the truth and prepare. Allow Jesus to be your Lord. Then watch as climate change occurs from a set in your heavenly home.

CHAPTER 13

It's Over: The Ark Has Settled

I struggled with how to end this. If you like, you can read the last three or four chapters in the Revelation. Jesus is now the King of kings and Lord of lords. You can also go back to Genesis and see that after the flood, the ark settled back on a different earth. There are all kinds of things to study and add to the timeline of God's word, but basically, climate change has happened for the second time, and we see it here in scripture.

I guess that we could say that we are beginning to see changes happening in our lives today. I can't say and truly don't know. I'm just a simple man, not very educated but seeking God's will for my life, a man who truly has a desire in my feeble way to help people to prepare to meet God.

When the ark settles, typically speaking, what do you think will be seen in the new heaven and new earth?

We can, in scripture, see some things and ponder those things. That is the joy: knowing where you will spend eternity and pondering and learning things that will be.

For instance, today, we have cell phones that are actually miniature computers. Remember, the two prophets were left dead in the streets for three days? I can see how cell phones can be used to show the world those men. It was a time we couldn't see how that was possible, but now we see it.

A while back, I heard a politician say that climate change would cause the disappearance of a lot of people. I thought, when I heard it, that the Antichrist could use climate change as a reason people disappeared at the rapture of the church. Of course, he would not be speaking of the real climate change but using what men think climate change is today. Can you see in that statement just how close the coming of Christ could be?

These things are things I think about. Actually, it's just my thought process as I look forward to the coming of Christ, the anticipation, trying to tie it all together. Are you looking for the coming of Christ? Did you know that there is a reward awaiting in heaven for those that love his appearing?

Henceforth there is laid up for me a crown of righteousness, which the Lord the righteous judge shall give me at that day; and not to me only but unto all them that love his appearing. (2 Timothy 4:8)

There are those who are born again, members of the body of Christ who are not excited about his return. There could be any number of reasons for that: sin in their life, love of this world, or simply being carnally minded. However, there are those who are looking for his return. What a blessing to have a heart for him!

When we consider this earth and other things after the next climate change, what will it be like?

The first thing to settle is that it will be here. It will be completely ruled by the King of kings and Lord of lords, Jesus Christ.

The Bible teaches us that God's chosen people, the nation of Israel, shall inherit the earth. We also see in the Revelation the city with one thousand five hundred square miles of pure gold, a home for the bride of Christ. These things are easily proven to those who believe. How it all comes together is hard for me to describe. Maybe other people can, and they can teach me. I'd love to understand more.

I believe there are two distinct places: that city for the bride of Christ and the earth, the home of God's people. These are things to be studied if you're interested.

I'd also like to point out something common to both the Garden of Eden and the new earth. That is the tree of life. We hear about the tree of the knowledge of good and evil in the Garden of Eden, but the tree of life that was there is seldom mentioned, but there nonetheless.

Look at these two verses:

> And out of the ground made the LORD God to grow every tree that is pleasant to the sight, and good for food; the tree of life also in the midst of the garden, and the tree of knowledge of good and evil. (Genesis 2:9)
>
> Then the LORD God said, "Behold, the man has become like one of Us, to know good and evil. And now, lest he put out his hand and take also of the tree of life, and eat, and live forever." (Genesis 3:22)

The same tree of life is mentioned in the Revelation.

> In the midst of the street of it, and on either side of the river, was there the tree of life, which bare twelve manner of fruits, and yielded her fruit every month and leaves of the tree were for the healing of the nations. (Revelation 22:2)

If you remember, after the first climate change, Noah's ark only had eight people who survived the flood. After this climate change, there will be nations, and we also know the nation of Israel will be on earth. Jesus Christ will be the King of kings and Lord of lords.

If we as individuals or mankind as a whole could come to the resolution that everything we see, even today, revolves around the nation of Israel and the fact that Jesus is their king, spiritual eyes could be opened. But that is not likely to happen. Without getting in any deeper and trying to end this with the completion of the next climate change, our relationship and where we stand, either as a nation or as an individual, depends entirely on our acceptance of Jesus Christ as our savior and how we view Israel.

Many people might argue that, but God told Abraham way back, even before he penned down the law and gave it to Moses, that Abraham's seed would be the seed of a great nation. He told him that the land, as far as the eye could see, would be theirs, and he made this statement, "I will bless them that bless you and curse them that curse you."

"I will bless them that bless thee, and curse them that curse thee; and in thee shall all the families of the earth be blessed" (Genesis 12:3).

We walk to and fro. We design and create many things and continue to move forward. Some things are good, and some are bad. Through it all, we see God's will unfolding before our very eyes, right in the days that we live.

In the last fifty years or so, it has been more visible than ever to those who truly seek to see it.

In my humble opinion, and that's all it is, things really started to set themselves in line when Israel became a sovereign nation again (May 14, 1948). We could go on and on if we choose to because it has no end as far as the study goes. The word of God has no top or bottom. Neither does it have sides. We can study forever and not come close to learning it all. The Bible tells us in the last chapter of John that if all that Jesus both done and said were recorded, the world wouldn't hold the books.

Jesus did many other things as well. If every one of them were written down, I suppose that even the whole world would not have room for the books that would be written.. Amen. (John 21:25)

The second vessel to bring about the salvation before the second climate change was the belief by the faith of a man, the man Christ Jesus. Now at this time, in this book on climate change, it's over. Climate change has occurred, and now that vessel has settled back on earth again. That, of course, is metaphorical, but the fact's image is better given in God's word.

You who read, continue to study and grow in the grace of our lord and savior Jesus Christ.

My main objective in all that I say through this is to create a thought and maybe a desire for the truth.

CHAPTER 14

Closing Thoughts: Truth

In closing, I would like to say just a few things about the truth. We live in a time of little faith toward God and a lot of confusion. God tells us in his word that he is not the author of confusion. "For God is not the author of confusion, but of peace, as in all churches of the saints" (1 Corinthians 14:33).

As you see here, confusion is not of God. We can use this verse here and not in the least, take it out of the context it's used in. At this point, this particular church was facing great confusion. The point is made, however, that no matter what the confusion is, God is not in it. There are only two real powers on the face of this earth; every person is controlled by one of them at all times. Even when we think we are acting independently, one of those two powers is actually guiding what we do.

The truth is what we need in our lives more than any other thing, whether we are willing to acknowledge that or not. We are either allowing ourselves to be led by the spirit of God or some other spirit. All other spirits are under the influence of Satan. The Bible tells us to try the spirits. "Beloved, believe not every spirit, but try the spirits whether they are of God: because many false prophets are gone out into the world" (1 John 4:1).

Everything you read or hear needs to be tried by the Word of God.

Do you realize that, in truth, there is not one person on the face of this earth today, nor has it ever been, other than Jesus Christ himself, that deserves salvation? Every person deserves damnation. We are all sinners and have fallen far short of what God expects us to be.

"They have all gone out of the way they are together become unprofitable there is none that doeth good no not one" (Romans 3:12).

The truth is that we need the presence of the Holy Spirit in this world to bring conviction to our sinful hearts so that we might call on Jesus for salvation. Mankind is hopelessly lost with no other way to salvation other than the blood of Christ.

Just as the ark in Noah's day was the only way to be saved, today Christ is the only way of salvation. "Neither is there salvation in any other: for there is none other name under heaven given among men, whereby we must be saved (Acts 4:12).

Sometimes the truth is not easily spoken and can be hard to accept. When we learn to listen to our hearts as his spirit speaks and then yield to the convicting power of the Spirit, then and only then can we be free.

There are all kinds of religions in this world; basically, there always have been. There's one thing in each of them that we can all agree on. Speaking of the truth as it relates to each person, we all must die. That is a cord that weaves through every religion. The only god in any religion whom we can speak of who actually had the power to die and raise his own self from the dead, whom I know of, is Jesus Christ, the true god of this universe in a body of flesh.

He is the only one who said, "I have the power to lay my life down and also to take it up again."

Therefore doth my Father love me, because I lay down my life, that I might take it again. No man taketh it from me, but I lay it down of myself. I have power to lay it down, and I have power to take it again. This commandment have I received of my Father. (John 10:17–18)

The truth is that you, no matter who you are, God, in the body of Jesus Christ, loves you just as you are. His spirit is at work right this minute and desires that you see yourself for what you are, just as he does. Right this minute, you, as an individual, is he speaking to your heart? What is he saying to you? Is he trying, at this moment, to reveal the truth to you?

That is the power of the spirit of God that wants to create climate change within your heart, even as you read. His desire is to make your heart his kingdom for eternity.

The truth is hidden in your willingness—to accept who you, as an individual, truly are and what you truly need. Once you see those needs in yourself, then God, by the power of the Holy Spirit, will do the rest.

It's not in any religion or man. No church has this power, but it's in the body of Jesus Christ. He says, he is the way, the truth, and the life. "Jesus saith unto him, I am the way, the truth, and the life: no man cometh unto the Father, but by me" (John 14:6).

Churches that genuinely preach the true Jesus Christ are churches that realize their true responsibility, and that is to reveal God's word by hearing the very voice of God. This comes by praying and earnestly seeking to hear God as he speaks through his word.

The truth is very close to you; it is as close as the Holy Spirit that speaks within your heart. The Holy Spirit speaks directly to your heart through and by God's word. He only deals in the truth. All you, me, or any other person has to do is admit that you hear it. Admit that to yourself. Believe. Once you do that, then you can step on the ark of security that came by faith in Jesus Christ. Once that happens, you can tell the world about your faith.

The one main difference between the flood, the people of Noah's day, and you is what is seen. If a person started to help build the ark with Noah or simply stepped inside to be saved, then all could see just what they did. With you, right at this moment, if you ask Christ to be your savior, then you will have to share it so that people might see the salvation that is within you.

The truth is God designed salvation that way that people like you and me would become his voice in this world today to share his gospel and his way of salvation.

That if thou shalt confess with thy mouth the Lord Jesus, and shalt believe in thine heart that God hath raised him from the dead, thou shalt be saved. For with the heart man believeth unto righteousness; and with the mouth confession is made unto salvation. (Romans 10:9–10)

Climate change that is made by God is going to happen again at some point. What we, as people, do to harm this earth or to save this earth actually has little to do with the actions of God. What we, as individuals, do in a spiritual light has all to do with the well-being of our eternal life. It also helps direct our children and families; even our friends will be affected.

Salvation is made and given freely to anyone who desires to have it. What it costs us, and the people we love, if we don't find that salvation will have an everlasting price that will never be paid.

All that is revealed in this book, and even this one chapter, is based solely on my faith in the word of God. I believe it to be true and necessary for our eternal souls and the knowledge it takes to prepare for what is ahead of us.

The responsibility of spiritual men and women ends at spreading the truth from God's word to the people around us. This is also true for any pastor or Sunday-school teacher to tell the truth, to live the truth each day to the best of their ability. The salvation of the soul of people then rests in the power of the Holy Spirit as he uses the truth that faithful people have shared.

When faithful people spread the truth, and the Holy Spirit uses that truth to draw conviction on a soul that is lost or living in sin, then the burden falls on that single individual to make the choice of whom they will yield themselves to as their lord.

As I've stated before, be wise, seek the truth, and know for certain where you stand with God. Prepare yourself, whatsoever it takes, for your own future and the coming climate change that was purposely made by God.

One day, you will be glad you did.